EMPATH

Survival and Healing Guide for Empaths and
Highly Sensitive People to Shield Yourself From
Negative Energies, Manage Your Empathy and
Develop Your Gift

Judith Yandell

JUDITH YANDELL

Copyright © 2018 Judith Yandell

All rights reserved.

In no way is it legal to reproduce, duplicate, or transmit any part of this document in either electronic means or in printed format. recording of this publication is strictly prohibited and any storage of this document is not allowed unless with written permission from the publisher. all rights reserved. The information provided herein is stated to be truthful and consistent, in that any liability, in terms of inattention or otherwise, by any usage or abuse of any policies, processes, or directions contained within is the solitary and utter responsibility of the recipient reader. under no circumstances will any legal responsibility or blame be held against the publisher for any reparation, damages, or monetary loss due to the information herein, either directly or indirectly. Respective authors own all copyrights not held by the publisher. The information herein is offered for informational purposes solely, and is universal as so. the presentation of the information is without contract or any type of guarantee assurance. The trademarks that are used are without any consent, and the publication of the trademark is without permission or backing by the trademark owner. all trademarks and brands within this book are for clarifying purposes only and are the owned by the owners themselves, not affiliated with this document.

EMPATH

TABLE OF CONTENTS

Introduction 9

Chapter 1:
Scheduling for Discipline 10
   Empath, Empathy, and HSPs 10
   Scientific Evidence 11
   Where Do Empaths Come From? 13
   Traits of Empaths 13
   Am I an Empath? 16

Chapter 2:
Living Your Life 19
   Self-Acceptance 19
   Prioritize Self-Care 20
   Set Boundaries and Make Rules 22
   Accept Negativity 22
   Beware of Addictions 22
   Do Good 24
   Go for Your Goals 24

Chapter 3:
Controlling Your Gift 25
   Be Your Own First Priority 25
   Build Fences, Not Walls 25
   Practice Separation 27
   Understand Your Own Emotions 28
   Release Responsibility 28
   Celebrate! 29

Chapter 4:
Overcoming Your Fears 30
   Social Anxiety 30
      Do You Have Social Anxiety? 31
      Overcoming Social Anxiety 31
      Social Anxiety Challenges 35
   Fear of Rejection 36
   Fear of Intimacy 36
      Tips for Empaths in Intimate Relationships 37
   Fear of Being Selfish 38

Chapter 5:
Energy Vampires 40
   Is an Energy Vampire Preying on You? 41
   Classifying the Species of Energy Vampires 42
      Narcissist Vampires 42
      Victim Vampires 43
      Rage Vampires 44
      Controlling Vampire 45
      Drama Queen/King Vampire 46

Monologue Vampires 46
Staking Your Energy Vampire..46
Antidotes for the Bite of an Energy Vampire.......................................48

Chapter 6:
Developing Your Skills..49
   Types of Empaths..49
   Finding a Mentor 51
   Practice Visualization..52
   Grounding Visualization 52
   Shielding Visualization 52
   Bond-Cutting Visualization 53
   Protective Animal Visualization 53
   Radio Visualization 54
   Meditate Daily 54
   Use Affirmations..56
   Empaths and the Pineal Gland..57
   Detoxifying the Pineal Gland 57
   Embrace Spirituality 60
   The Journey of Enhancing and Developing Your Empath Skills 60
      Stage 1: Burdened with the Weight of the World......................61
      Stage 2: Embracing Self-Care 61
      Stage 3: Research and Experimentation.....................................61
      Stage 4: Training 61
      Stage 5: Skill Management 62
      Stage 6: Emotional Clarity 62
      Stage 7: Life Goes On 62

Chapter 7:
Wielding Your Gift 64
   Strategize 64
   Stop Problems While They Are Still Small 64
   Improve Your Personal Relationships...65
   Improve Your Work 65
   Brace Yourself..66
   Help Someone..67
   Crisis Hotlines..68
      The Peace Corps..68
      Fostering Animals 69
   Finding Fulfillment in Your Career...69
   What is Meaningful to You? 70
      Consider Your Co-workers' Energy 71
      Consider the Workplace's Energy..72

Chapter 8:
Loving an Empath 73
   Raising an Empath 73
      Is My Child an Empath? 73
      Understanding and Supporting Your Empathic Child 75
      Even Children Can Be Energy Vampires 78

    Teach by Example 79
    Open Mind, Open Heart, Open Communication 79
    Accept Yourself 80
    Intimate Relationship with an Empath 80

Chapter 9:
Affirmations for Empaths 83
    Guided Meditation 1 84
    Guided Meditation 2 88

Conclusion 93

EMPATH

JUDITH YANDELL

Introduction

The following chapters will discuss what an empath is and how it is different from being an empathetic person. In today's culture, empaths are sometimes portrayed as supernatural beings with magical powers or as New Age flakes. These are shortsighted interpretations of a natural gift. It may not be a gift you asked for or a gift you even want, but if you learn to harness and wield it, you will come to appreciate not only your abilities as an empath, but also your mind, body, and spirituality as a whole.

Being an empath can be difficult; you may have to deal with erroneous stereotypes, but you must keep in mind that it is a blessing. We will discuss how to accept yourself as an empath and develop your gifts, as well as control it in situations that could be too overwhelming otherwise. You will receive practical advice on how to live a normal life with your ability. We will delve into how to identify energy vampires that prey on empaths and how to protect yourself from them.

Although some people doubt the existence of empaths, there is scientific evidence that they exist. Even being an empath, you may doubt the extent that the abilities can manifest themselves, and that's fine. I only ask that you read this book with an open mind and an open heart. You may just come to understand yourself a little better and love yourself a little more.

There are plenty of books on this subject on the market, so thanks again for choosing this one! Every effort was made to ensure it is full of as much useful information as possible. Enjoy!

Chapter 1:
Scheduling for Discipline

"Could a greater miracle take place than for us to look through each other's eyes for an instant?"

Henry David Thoreau (1817-1862)

Empath, Empathy, and HSPs

Being an empath is frequently interpreted simply as a person who is very empathetic. Although empaths have high levels of empathy, it goes much further than this. The Oxford Dictionary defines empathy as "the ability to understand and share the feelings of another." Empaths not only share the feelings of others, but they experience the feelings as if they are their own.

Highly Sensitive People (HSPs) have intense physical, mental, and emotional reactions to stimuli. While most empaths share this intense reaction to stimuli, being an empath goes beyond this as well. It is the ability to sense and absorb energy, whether it be positive or negative, from other people and your surroundings. While HSPs feel better after they are no longer exposed to overwhelming stimuli, empaths will take longer to recover.

While being empathetic, particularly to the degree an empath experiences can be draining, it is certainly a positive trait. Consider this, the opposite of an empath are people with Narcissistic Personality Disorder. NPDs are classified as people who are unable to feel empathy. Going even further, we find sociopaths and psychopaths who lack both empathy and the ability to feel normal human emotions.

Scientific Evidence

Unless you are an empath, you can't truly know what is going on in someone's mind and body. Therefore, it is very difficult to prove or disprove the existence of empaths. However, scientists are working on it and have found evidence, though it is indirect. You can study the brain of empaths versus non-empaths; you can do studies on people who claim to be empaths. Although these studies can help us to understand empaths, they are hampered by people who claim to be empaths but are confused by what exactly it means to be empathic or are simply lying about their abilities.

Everyone has mirror neurons in their brain. These neurons allow humans to feel compassion towards themselves, other people, animals, and the environment. Mirror neurons facilitate the interpretation of people's emotion by filtering them through our own emotions. The mirror neurons of empaths are hypersensitive compared to that of an average person. This hypersensitivity allows empaths to sense the emotions of others and also to absorb the energy of others and their surroundings.

Abigail Marsh[1] has done studies on psychopaths, which are considered the opposite of empaths. Marsh compared the brains of psychopaths with a control group. She showed both groups pictures of people with frightened facial expressions. The control group was better at recognizing the fear expressed than the psychopathic group and were more responsive to it. The amygdala[2] of the control group was approximately 18% larger than that of the psychopathic group.
Marsh then selected a group of people that had anonymously donated kidneys, an extremely altruistic act. In her study, she labels

---

[1] Marsh, Abigail. *The Fear Factor: How One Emotion Connects Altruists, Psychopaths & Everyone In-Between*. New York: Basic Books, 2017.

[2] Amygdala is a cluster of neurons in the brain's temporal lobe that has a key role in processing emotions.

them as "anti-psychopaths." Although she doesn't use the term "empath", her descriptions of them align with traits commonly found in empaths. Her finding showed that, in comparison with the control group, the anti-psychopaths were better able to recognize facial expressions denoting fear and were more responsive to it. The amygdala of the anti-psychopaths was found to be 8% larger than the amygdala of the control group.

Marsh's study doesn't prove beyond a reasonable doubt, but it provides empirical evidence that anti-psychopaths have a stronger than average ability to recognize emotions expressed by others and have stronger reactions to the emotions they witness. This difference is even more distinct when comparing the results between anti-psychopaths and psychopaths. Marsh discovered there is a measurable difference in their brain between anti-psychopaths, the control group, and psychopaths.

Electromagnetic fields are naturally found in the heart and brain. These fields transmit thoughts and emotions. Empaths can simply tune in to these electromagnetic fields more accurately than an average person can. Some empaths have reported being able to experience the emotion of someone they know well, even when there is a great distance between them. They have already accessed the person's electromagnetic field, and if the emotion is strong enough, it can be transmitted despite long distances.

Dopamine is a neurotransmitter that helps to control the brain's reward and pleasure center. It also plays a part in the regulation of emotions. Empaths have been found to experience dopamine differently than other people. Studies have shown that empaths are more sensitive to the effects of dopamine that the rest of the population. It has also been found that empaths are more sensitive to dopamine. They need less than an average person to feel happy.

There is a huge amount of anecdotal evidence supporting the existence of empaths: people who report knowing that a loved one is in pain or has passed away before they are told; and people who can sense that something wonderful or horrible has happened in specific locations that they know nothing about.

Where Do Empaths Come From?

They are born with the ability. Some people are born with better vision than others. Some are born blind. In the same way, empaths are born with a stronger connection to their senses and the ability to feel the emotions of others. The tendency to be overly sensitive to external stimuli can sometimes be noticeable from birth; the child may be especially sensitive to light, sound, and being touched.

It's in their genes. Studies have shown that multiple empaths tend to be found in the same family line. It can pass along both the maternal and paternal lines.

It develops from a traumatic experience. People who were abused or neglected as a child don't develop the same defenses as most people. This can heighten their sensitivity to experiencing emotions of others because they are not forming the same mental and emotional boundaries as their peers. This is particularly common when the parents have real issues, such as Narcissist Personality Disorder, alcoholism, or drug addiction. The child will often blame themselves for their parent's actions and develop low self-esteem. If you have developed empath abilities in this manner, self-care will be particularly important for you. Please remember, ***it is not your fault***. No child should suffer. But the suffering brought you a gift. Use it to help others that were in similar situations.

Positive parenting can also amplify empath traits that you were born with, augmenting them. Perhaps as a child, you really bonded with plants. Your parents may have nurtured that quality and given you a corner of their yard to take care of. As a result of this nurturing and encouragement, you may have developed into a plant empath (see Chapter 6 for information about the different types of empaths). If your natural inclination had not been nurtured, your abilities might have remained latent.

Traits of Empaths

Although empaths are all unique individuals and can be found in all locations and cultures throughout the world, they share certain personality traits.

Sensitivity to Other People
Empaths are open, generous, and great listeners. They are considered nurturers; they want to help others and make the people around them happy. Empaths are very altruistic; they continue to give without expecting anything back. Empaths are very prone to having their feelings hurt. Many people who characterize themselves as empaths report they are often criticized for being too sensitive.

Increased Sensitivity to Stimuli
Many empaths are also Highly Sensitive People (HSPs). Their five senses are highly tuned and can lead to sensory overload. They tend to avoid crowds and intensely dislike loud noises.

Generosity
Having a "big heart" is a common way empaths are described. They want to help others, and in doing so, often take on the pain or suffering they are trying to alleviate in others.

Extremely Empathetic
Empaths can feel the emotion of others and absorb it. They experience these emotions as their own. For example, if a person is grieving for a lost loved one, an empathetic person will truly feel sad for the grieving person and would want to support them. However, an empath will actually experience the same feelings of grief to the same degree, as if they were grieving for someone themselves.

Introversion
Many empaths, though not all, are introverts. Experiencing the emotions of others can be extremely draining, so many empaths tend to prefer the company of themselves or small groups of people to large gatherings. It is important to remember that introverts are not necessarily shy or socially awkward. Many introverts are perfectly charming and lead healthy and active social lives. It simply means that an introvert needs alone time to relax and decompress after these events.

High Levels of Intuition
Empaths pick up on subtle clues and energies that most people miss. They might not know exactly why they feel a certain way about a person, but they should trust themselves. If an empath tells you to be wary of a certain person, heed that warning

Wariness of Intimate Relationships
Many empaths may avoid intimate relationships. It is easy for an empath to feel overwhelmed by a person they spend a lot of time with, particularly when there is a deep connection. With the physical closeness and the amount of time spent together in intimate relationships, empaths fear that their desire to give to others will deplete them. They also worry that the emotions of their partner will subsume their own emotions. We will discuss later in this book how empaths can maintain their sense of self while in relationships.

Extreme Vulnerability to Energy Vampires
Empaths and energy vampires tend to be drawn to one another. Despite this attraction, this is not a healthy relationship for the empath. They want to give and energy vampires want to take. Spending too much time around an energy vampire can be mentally, physically, and emotionally draining to an empath.

Kindness
A jaded person might refer to an empath as a "doormat," but the truth is that empaths cannot bear to hurt others, even when it is in self-defense. Empaths tend not to stand up for themselves against cruel words or actions of others. This is not because they are weak or defenseless; they are deciding to not react in a retaliatory nature. Beyond just being incredibly kind, they feel what others feel. Therefore, they don't want to hurt anyone.

Nurtured by Nature
Many empaths feel that being in nature is relaxing, grounding, and reviving. It helps them release their tension and unburden themselves.

Nurturer by Nature
Empaths often find that they are sought out by people in need. While empaths can sense when people are in pain, people often sense that interactions with empaths will make them feel better. Empaths may find that they are the go-to person for advice among their friends, family, and co-workers. Instinctively knowing what to say or do to help someone is a quality that empaths share.

Am I an Empath?

Many people describe themselves as having traits similar to an empath: nice, likes nature, introvert, kind, generous. If you are reading this, you likely already suspect that you are an empath, and you may have many of the qualities of an empath. But how do you know if you are really an empath? Here's a little text to help you find out more. Please read this list of phrases and count the number of statements you identify with.

- I know how people are feeling. I can tell when someone is struggling, even when they are covering up their feelings with their words and body language.

- I can tell when someone is lying to me.

- People gravitate to me. Not only the people in my daily life, but random people strike up conversations with me. I frequently find myself in deep conversations with people in line at stores, as they tell me their life story.

- I love alone time. I do not enjoy being social. It makes me feel tired, dirty, and confused.

- I love alone time. Even though I enjoy being social, I crave time alone, which rejuvenates, refreshes, and relaxes me.

- I know things intuitively. I usually know who is on the phone before I answer it. Sometimes, I even know someone is calling before the phone rings. When I was in school, I would forget to study sometimes, but I knew the answers anyway. I could almost always predict when there would be a pop quiz!

- I feel emotions that do not correlate with my own life. I sometimes feel random spurts of joy, depression, and anger that have nothing to do with what I am experiencing.

- I can feel the emotions of animals, as well as easily calm an anxious animal that I have never met before.

- I love to be outside. Whether it be a long hike or working on my garden, this gives me energy and helps me to relax.

- I find large crowds or groups overwhelming and would rather socialize in small groups.

- The news, horror movies, and medical dramas are TV programs I tend to avoid as they are too depressing. It takes me a long time to cheer up if I watch one of these programs.

- I feel exhausted after spending time in crowds, even if I had a great time.

- I avoid intimate relationships.

- I find multitasking to be overwhelming.

- I prefer the suburbs and rural settings to cities.

- I experience sensory overload. I avoid places like food courts, perfume stores, malls, and movie theaters. They make me dizzy, anxious, and exhausted.

- I often feel that I don't fit in and that people don't relate to me. But this doesn't stop them from telling me all their problems!

- I feel emotionally and physically exhausted after talking to my friend who always needs my help and always has problems, but never seems to reciprocate the support I give them.

- I feel unclean after I have to touch a lot of people, no matter how clean these people are!

- I feel like I absorb the emotions of others. After spending time with a person who is sad, it takes me a long time to cheer up. When I spend time with someone joyful, I feel joyful as well, even if my own life isn't going so well.

If you agree with 1-5 of these statements, you have some qualities of an empath.

If you agree with 6-10 of these statements, you have moderate qualities of an empath.

If you agree with 11-15 of these statements, you have high levels of qualities of an empath.

If you agree with 16-20 of these statements, congratulations, you are definitely an empath!

If you did not score as high as you would like, you could still work to develop your skills as an empath. You may not have the same natural abilities as some, but you can hone and strengthen the abilities that you have. For example, you may never be able to tell how an animal is feeling, but it would certainly be worthwhile to enhance your tendency to intuit when someone is lying to you.

Chapter 2:
Living Your Life

Some empaths turn to drugs or alcohol to numb their abilities and make it easier to function, while others may isolate themselves to prevent their talents from manifesting. They are doing themselves and the people who care about them a disservice. Yes, being an empath can be difficult; but it is a wonderful talent that you can learn to embrace and control so that you can lead a normal, happy, productive, and uniquely talented life!

Self-Acceptance

"Our innate capacity for empathy is the source of the most precious of all human qualities."

His Holiness the 14th Dalai Lama

Empaths may feel that they have been cursed with their ability. They tire of people telling them to "toughen up" or critically telling them "don't be so sensitive." In today's culture, being sensitive is a highly undervalued trait, while it seems like narcissism rules. However, being sensitive is not a weakness. Being kind and generous is not a weakness. These qualities take a lot of strength. It is not a showy strength, but an innate power. It is the type of strength that will support you throughout your entire life.

Many people feel confusion, anger, and isolation before they recognize and accept their empathic abilities. It can be particularly upsetting for children who feel intense emotions that they do not have the experiences and maturity to understand. Think about how scary it would be to a child that is experiencing the emotions of their parents going through a divorce. However, once you have recognized the abilities in yourself, you can begin to understand and control them, so they do not overwhelm your life and you can finally embrace and use them.

Prioritize Self-Care

Putting themselves first can be a huge struggle for empaths. But to care for others, you must first care for yourself. You cannot give if you have nothing left to give. For empaths, time alone is a huge component of self-care. Although as an empath you can and should strive to lead a normal life (go to work, have friends, and socialize) you will need more time than most to decompress. You absorb the emotions and energy of those around you, and you need time and space for yourself to release that energy and those emotions.

Empaths tend to love water. Try taking a nice hot bath at least once a week with Epsom salt, which is a natural detoxifier.

Meditation and yoga can be very helpful at relaxing and rejuvenating your mind, body, and soul. You can take classes, use apps, or follow online videos. It is important to remember that yoga and meditation are referred to as practices for a reason. They will not work immediately. It takes time, but practicing these regularly will have a cumulative effect on your mind and body.

Strenuous exercise can also be great at both clearing your mind and improving your mood. Exercise increases your body's level of endorphins, which are naturally-produced hormones that make you feel happy. Go for a walk, a run, or try an exercise class. Before beginning a new exercise regime, discuss your plans with your doctor. If you are a beginner, make sure you start slow and build your way up. You don't want to get an injury.

Spend time in nature. Most empaths feel a true connection with nature. Take a hike, do some yard work, take pictures of plants, or spend some time by a body of water. Go for a swim if it is warm and safe enough.

Unplug! The influx of information in today's technological world can be overwhelming to anyone. Compound that with the sensitivities of an empath, and it is downright exhausting. Turn off your phone. Stop checking your social media. Instead of scrolling through your feed, read a book or listen to music. Choose mindfulness activities overlooking through mind-numbing posts.

Start a journal. Get all your feelings, frustrations, and worries out on paper. Acknowledge them, accept them, and dismiss them. The very act of writing down how you feel can be very cathartic.

Get enough sleep. The more tired you are, the more easily and quickly you will be drained by other people and your surroundings.

Listen to your body. You know what makes you feel better. You may feel more energized after a nap than a run. If you don't like getting dirty, don't garden. Find other ways to experience nature. Keep trying different methods until you find what works for you, and keep an open mind throughout the process.

Adopt a pet. If you have the space, funds, and time for a pet, look into adopting one. If you do not have time for training, you can get an adult cat or dog. The unconditional love that a pet gives can be very soothing for an empath. You get to care for something that asks nothing from you other than love, food, and shelter, and gives you love, companionship, and loyalty in return.

Take a retreat. If you are financially able, take the time to go on a retreat once a year. Find a place where you can be in nature, have peace and quiet, and fully decompress. Use this time to tune into yourself and your needs. Immerse yourself in the experience. Only check your phone once a day in case of emergencies in the outside world. Pick a location that speaks to you. The mountains, by a lake or the ocean, and in forests are great places to start looking. You can participate in a planned retreat, or you can do it yourself. A major benefit to a planned retreat is that you don't have to worry about cooking for yourself!

Set Boundaries and Make Rules

There may be some people or situations in your life that you would be happier to avoid. But you should not use this as an excuse to avoid your life! It is important to find a balance of having a social life and being functional in the workplace, while not becoming completely overwhelmed. You may not be able to cut toxic people, otherwise known as energy vampires, out of your life completely, but you can limit the time you spend with them. In the next chapter, we will discuss more in depth how to set boundaries with those in your life.

Express your needs. If you are sensitive to loud noises, implement a no-yelling rule in your home. Suggest it at work as well. The emotions and sensory overload that occurs with yelling is often overwhelming and draining for an empath. Request that anger is expressed healthily. Make sure everyone knows that this does not mean they need to hide what is bothering them. Instead of yelling, they should take time to calm down so they can express themselves healthily and constructively.

Accept Negativity

If you expect to be happy all the time, you will either live in a state of disappointment or denial. If you are sad, it is ok to be sad. If you lose a loved one, take the time to grieve. By acknowledging the negative aspects of your life, you are better able to process them and move on. Denial does not make anything go away. It is a form of procrastination that you will have to deal with eventually. It is easier to deal with negatively when the experience is causing it is happening, rather than let it become pent up for weeks or even years.

Beware of Addictions

Because empaths are often overstimulated and overwhelmed, they tend to self-medicate with alcohol, drugs, food, and sex. Except for drugs, there is nothing wrong with these if done safely and moderately. However, using them to numb your senses and the pain you feel through others can be dangerous. Alcohol and drugs are often used by empaths to protect themselves from being overwhelmed in crowds. It dulls how strongly they feel their own emotions and numbs their ability to experience the emotions of others.

Using addiction as a coping mechanism has many ill effects in the long term. It can put you at risk for disease, depression, and even death. They exhaust your body and shut down your abilities as an empath. Although they keep you from being overwhelmed in the short term, your mind and body will be worn down in the long run and you will struggle even more in protecting yourself from being overwhelmed by excessive stimuli.

Although drugs and alcohol are the most recognized and easily diagnosed addictions, be aware of others as well. Have you ever been late for work or school because you are playing video games excessively? Do the people around you consistently ask you to put down your phone and turn off social media? Is your shopping habit causing you to struggle financially? Be careful of anything that you do on a regular basis to shut off your feelings and protect yourself from the world that prevents you from living a happy, healthy, and fulfilled life.

You are not being advised to lead a monastic lifestyle. If you are using moderation and activities are enhancing your life instead of taking it over, you can indulge yourself. If you have had a bad day (are 21 or over and not an alcoholic) there is nothing wrong with relaxing over a glass of wine. If it's your birthday and you have the funds available, treat yourself to a shopping trip. If you broke up with your partner, eat as much ice cream and pizza as you want to that night.

If you have an addiction, do not try to beat it by yourself. Ask for help. It is not something to be ashamed of. Don't blame yourself or your gift you are trying to numb. Be proud of yourself for recognizing the problem and taking proactive steps to fix it. Join a Twelve-Step Program. Allow yourself to be inspired by people in the program who have overcome their addictions. Listen to their advice. Learn to control your abilities in positive ways. We will discuss this in Chapter 6.

Do Good

Empaths love to help people. It makes them happy to make others happy. Harness your positive energy into charities that are especially meaningful to you. If you love animals, volunteer for the ASPCA. If you love to cook, find a local soup kitchen at which to volunteer; if there isn't one, start one! If you love kids, look into being a mentor. Many worthy organizations would benefit greatly from your time and gifts.

Not everyone has the time to volunteer. You don't just have to participate in organizations to do good in the world. There are simple things you can do in your day-to-day life. Make dinner for an elderly neighbor. Pick up trash when you're going for walks. If your friend is going through a breakup, bring them wine, ice cream, and a shoulder to cry on. Compliment a stranger. Little things can go a surprisingly long way in making the people around you feel valued.

Go for Your Goals

Although helping others is wonderful, it is important to remember your own goals. Empaths tend to use an inordinate amount of their energy on other people. But you are valuable too! Your goals are worth reaching! Write down your short-term and long-term goals. Look at them every day. Strategize ways to achieve your goals. Journal about your setbacks and progress.

Chapter 3:
Controlling Your Gift

"I believe empathy is the most essential quality of civilization."

Roger Ebert (1942-2013)

Be Your Own First Priority

If you are completely drained, you will not be able to deal with the struggles of daily life or handle normal interactions with people. Even a person who's not an empath will struggle to control their emotions when they are exhausted and depleted. This is much worse for empaths, as they are dealing with their own emotions, as well as the emotions of the people and energy around them. Please see Chapter 2 for tips on self-care. Putting yourself first is not a selfish act. This is difficult for empaths to accept, but when they put this into practice, they will realize its importance.

Build Fences, Not Walls

Empaths tend to isolate themselves to prevent being overwhelmed by the emotions and energies of others. Don't do this! By all means, take time alone to decompress when you need to, but there is no reason that you can't have a healthy, active social life and be successful at work.

You can and should support the people in your life. However, it is important that you do not give them all your energy. You will be a better friend and a family member and lead a more meaningful life if you are not depleted. To accomplish this, you need to develop boundaries.

If you have a coworker who is draining for you to be around, you can still work with them. But you do not need to socialize outside of the workplace. If they invite you to lunch, politely decline. Use the excuse that you have to work for lunch. Next time, tell them that you brought lunch or you are on a special diet. They will eventually get the hint. Keep your interactions with co-workers you find draining limited to what is necessary for your job. On days that you know you'll need to spend a lot of time with them for professional reasons, take some extra time for yourself in the morning to practice self-care. Make sure you take the time that evening to decompress.

If you feel your life would be better without a certain person in your life, you should cut them out of your life. For example, you may have a friend from your childhood that always needs something from you and always has problems they want you to solve, but is who never there for you in return. Someone like this can be extremely draining for anyone to maintain a friendship with but is even more difficult for an empath. Empaths have a harder time saying no. It is harder to cut a conversation short. But if someone is bringing toxicity into your life, don't feel that you have to keep them in it just because you have a shared history. If this feels too selfish, try to reframe how you think about it: you will have a lot of time and energy to help other people if this toxic person is no longer in your life. Your friend will be better off if they have a friend without empathic abilities who is not so drained being around them. They can find another toxic person, and they can be toxic together.

For people, such as family members that you cannot cut out of your life, you should set clearly-defined boundaries. For example, you may have a sister who you love dearly, but who is so needy that you always feel very drained after interacting with her. In this example, you could set boundaries such as limiting the time you spend with the person or on the phone. Your boundaries may be that you end your daily phone call after ten minutes and schedule a two-hour brunch every other week. Your boundaries should be based on your relationship with the person and how much interacting with them drains you.

At a certain time each evening, turn off your phone or at least silence the ringer. Let your friends and family know that after this time of night, you are unavailable, except in emergencies. Don't be afraid to tell them that you consider an emergency a health crisis or similar. Your younger sister's fifteenth breakup with the same man she keeps going back to is not an emergency under this paradigm. You can talk to her about this the next day during your ten-minute phone call. You can support the people in your life and be there for them without being at the beck and call.

Many empaths find that touch intensifies the emotions they are experiencing through others and increases energy absorption. When you are in a crowd, you can try to navigate the edges, so you aren't bumping into as many people. You can give shorter hugs when you greet friends. You don't want to close yourself off completely to touch, but some people are just not as physically affectionate as others. Being one of them is fine. If you are meeting a lot of new people and want to avoid shaking hands, mention you feel like you have a cold coming on. People will appreciate the warning and keep their hands to themselves. Once you learn to shield yourself, you will not have to worry about making these excuses.

If you are in a social situation and are feeling intense vibes from someone that are making you uncomfortable or upset, you can move away. Do this kindly and unobtrusively. No one will think your behavior is odd or antisocial if you politely excuse yourself to refill a beverage, get some food, or use the restroom. If you are in a waiting room, you can always move seats. Grab your things, make a phone call outside, or ask the receptionist a question. When you return, simply sit elsewhere. Most people self-absorbed enough to not even notice.

Practice Separation

Empaths feel the emotions of others as strongly as they do their own. But it is important to remember that these emotions you are feeling through others aren't yours. They don't reflect what you are experiencing in your life. If your best friend is going through a divorce, the anger and sadness you are feeling through them is not your anger and sadness. Be there for your friend. Do your best to help and support them, but do not let their situation subsume you.

To practice separation, you first need to acknowledge the emotions you are feeling. Then, you mentally compartmentalize them as belonging to your friend and release them. Allow yourself to decompress and clear your mind after interacting with this friend. Try the self-care tips mentioned in Chapter 2 to help you clear your mind.

Understand Your Own Emotions

Once you have separated the emotions you are experiencing through other people, it's time to concentrate on your own emotions. We'll continue with the example of an empath who has a friend going through a divorce. When you have released the anger and sadness you are feeling through them, think about your relationship. Do you have a significant other? How do you feel about the relationship? Does your partner make you happy and enhance your life? If you are single, are you content with this or do you want a relationship? What do you need and want in a partner? What do you expect to get out of being in a relationship?

Discover how you are feeling in your own life. Acknowledge and understand your emotions. Determine the source of these emotions. If you are sad, figure out why. Sometimes, the source will be obvious; other times, you will have to delve deeper. When you are more aware of your life and emotions, it will make it easier for you to separate your emotions from the emotions you feel through other people. Journaling can be a great way to examine your emotions, as well as practicing separation.

Are you happy? What can make you happier? Are you depressed? Why? What can you do to make it better? You give so much support to the people in your life; don't be afraid to ask them for support if you need it! You may decide you would benefit from therapy to further explore your emotions.

Release Responsibility

Empaths often feel they carry the weight of the world. They burden themselves with the suffering and problems of others. Empaths feel extreme guilt for not being able to fix other people's problems. You are not responsible for other people's problems. It's not your fault your best friend is struggling through a divorce. You cannot fix it. You would be overstepping your bounds to attempt to do so. You must let those around you live their own life and make their own decisions. This includes letting them make their own mistakes. You can actually do people a disservice by not allowing them to fend for themselves. They need to learn to rely on themselves and their own strength, not just yours. Concentrate on your own life and your own path.

If it is hard for you to change your mindset from fixing people to supporting them, consider that by controlling your empath abilities, you are allowing the people in your life to have privacy. You wouldn't want someone to read your every emotion. You can consider shielding a form of respect.

If you receive information through intuition that you feel it's imperative to share, be respectful of how the other person receives your information. You may get a bad feeling around your friend's significant other. If you choose to share this with your friend, be prepared that they won't want to hear it and they may be angry with you for telling them. You can tell them why you feel this way, but don't tell them what to do.

Celebrate!

There is a lot of pain and sadness in the world. This can weigh particularly heavily on empaths, who experience so much emotional pain that is not their own. Don't wait for holidays to celebrate the good things, whether large or small. Take the time to celebrate and bring joy into your life and the lives of those around you. If you got a promotion at work, treat yourself to a nice dinner. If you accomplished a workout goal, buy yourself a new training outfit. Is your 40th birthday coming up? Throw yourself a birthday bash! No "over the hill" paraphernalia allowed—good vibes only! Host a dinner party just because you have a new recipe you want to try.

Chapter 4:
Overcoming Your Fears

If you're enjoying the book, make sure to go to Amazon and leave a short review. I would love to hear your thoughts.

Social Anxiety

Due to how overwhelming it can be for empaths to be in large groups, particularly children who don't understand what they are experiencing, many develop social anxiety. First of all, realize that this is completely normal and not a weakness. It is a challenge that will make you stronger in the long run. Millions of people have social anxiety, and the majority is not even empaths. Empaths pick up on any toxic energy and emotions that are in the crowd. You would be hard-pressed to find a large group of people who were all only emoting positivity. Although you may choose to see a therapist to help you through social anxiety, there are also things you can do on your own. These suggestions should not replace or interfere with what a therapist tells you to do but can be used as supplements.

Social anxiety is an irrational level of stress about interacting with other people and the preoccupation with how people are judging you. It leads to feeling embarrassed, inadequate, and extremely self-conscious. Experiencing an irrational level of stress makes you an irrational person. It is important to face your social anxiety and try to improve upon it, as empaths tend to be introverted, to begin with.

The majority of people have situations that make them nervous or uncomfortable. Being nervous occasionally is normal; it doesn't mean you have social anxiety. Your nervousness becomes an issue when it prevents you from doing things you would otherwise like to do, such as going to a party, or would be beneficial to your life, such as leading an important presentation at work. Social anxiety can manifest itself with physical symptoms, such as flushing in the face, neck, and ears, trembling, nausea, and sweating.

Do You Have Social Anxiety?

Check the following statements if they apply to you:

- I often avoid social situations because I feel I'm being judged.

- My anxiety in social situations often manifests itself with physical symptoms.

- The physical symptoms create a vicious cycle, making me even more anxious. I know people are judging me for them!

- My anxiety about social situations regularly affects my family, work, friendships, and romantic relationships.

- I dread one-on-one conversations with people I don't know well.

- I rarely feel comfortable interacting with a group of strangers.

- I often use my phone as a shield to avoid participating in conversations.

- I frequently use alcohol or other substances to help me feel more at ease in a social situation.

If you have checked two or more of these, you likely have social anxiety. But don't despair! Identifying the issue is the first step to fixing it.

Overcoming Social Anxiety

The following methods are tailored to help empaths with social anxiety; however, with slight modifications, they can also benefit non-empaths. If you choose to seek therapy for your social anxiety, please let your therapist know that you're an empath or have qualities of an empath. This will help them to adjust your cognitive behavioral therapy to best help you. You may even find that your therapist is an empath too! Many empaths are drawn to this line of work.

Imagine the worst-case scenario. When you have come up with an extremely negative outcome, analyze the likelihood that this could happen. If you have a presentation coming up at work, your worst-case scenario could be that you would open your mouth to begin, regurgitate your last meal, and be fired. When you think about it in this manner, you will realize that the actual likelihood of this happening is absurdly low. Now that you considered and rejected the extreme, rationally think about the most likely outcome. You may stutter a few times or not keep eye contact; nothing that will get you fired or even reprimanded. Keep in mind that this is your area of expertise. People are attending the presentation to hear what you have to say for a reason, and it is not to see you fail. To take a pessimistic view of people, they would consider it a waste of their time.

Use your nervous energy to prepare. Practice your upcoming presentation. Do it in front of the mirror. Give the presentation to your spouse. Use your self-care techniques the morning of your presentation so that you are as relaxed as possible. Before the presentation, try to get some alone time, when you can separate the emotions you are feeling through other people from your own. Your nervousness is enough to deal with; don't compound it with the negative emotions of others. If you have a coworker who's consistently happy and confident, try to spend some time with them right before the presentation. Embrace their emotions and positive energy. Avoid the negative people, if possible.

Change your thought patterns. People with social anxiety tend to have a negative, cyclical way of thinking about social situations. For example, the more stressed you are, the more likely you are to have physical symptoms. This gives you even more to worry about. You may begin the conversation already stressed, but then, as you analyze everything you are saying in a conversation, you reprimand yourself and think of how you could have said it better. Try to stop and think rationally. You may have stuttered a couple of times during a conversation. Would you judge someone for stuttering? Is it really a big deal? Remind yourself that as an empath, you are naturally a good listener. Try to concentrate on being a good listener, rather than focusing on judging yourself. This should come naturally to you!

It can be helpful to remember that as much as you are judging yourself, the people you are interacting with are likely doing the same thing. Unfortunately, for an empath, this means that they are absorbing this energy from the people around them. This is an instance in which getting in the habit of practicing separation of your emotions from the emotions of others will be important.

Are you only thinking about what you did wrong? Perhaps you were blushing when you told a funny joke that got a great reaction. Stop thinking about the blush and think about how people enjoyed the joke!

Are you focused too much on the past? Were you made fun of in school? Well, you're an adult now; you are no longer that awkward preteen. You don't judge others by how they were when they were younger, so why would they judge you like that? More importantly, why would you judge yourself like that? Think of all you have accomplished and how much you have changed.

People often say that you should treat others the way you would treat yourself. But, as an empath, you should treat yourself the way you would treat others—with compassion, kindness, and generosity.

It takes time and patience to change your negative thought patterns. You don't have to be completely positive at all times. Just try to be rational and logical in the way you are thinking.

Change your behaviors. Do you have certain crutches that you use in social situations? Maybe you are always checking your phone. You might have a couple of friends that you cling to when you are at an event. Take the time to reflect on what you do in social situations. You probably crutch that you don't even realize. Write them down. Journal about how you could stop using them altogether or alter them. Most importantly, begin implementing these ideas.

Desensitize yourself. Gradually expose yourself to more situations that give you social anxiety. Do this slowly, so you don't become overwhelmed. If one of your social crutches is a group of friends that you don't branch out from, start by trying to socialize with other people at an event while they are there. You still have your support system to fall back on if necessary. Eventually, you can go to social events that your support group is not attending. Ridding yourself of this crutch doesn't mean you have to give up your friends! You are simply expanding your comfort level with others.

You may never like large social events. There is nothing wrong with that, but you can handle attending them when necessary or beneficial. There's no reason for you not to have an active and healthy social life. Take the initiative and plan smaller events with your close friends and family.

Our goal is to go against your inclination to avoid social situations. You may never feel completely comfortable with certain social groups and situations, but you will be better equipped to handle them when they arise. You may never enjoy large, loud, meetings at work. But if other than those meetings you love your job, you can teach yourself to be able to handle it.

Use visualization. Empaths tend to be daydreamers. Harness that natural inclination, visualize the social situation you are dreading, and how you will handle yourself. Visualize yourself giving a fantastic presentation at work. Visualize yourself socializing with people you don't know at a party. Think about the insightful comments you will make and the interesting topics you'll bring up.

Your skills as an empath will make overcoming social anxiety harder for you than the average person. Remember that you are not average —you have an exceptional skill! Conquering your social anxiety will make you an even stronger person. If you and your trained medical professional decide that an anti-anxiety medicine is right for you and your social anxiety, this is nothing to be ashamed of. You are using the tools you have at your disposal to help yourself live a more healthy and well-rounded life. Consider this: would you judge someone else for taking anti-anxiety medications? Of course not. Don't judge yourself either.

Social Anxiety Challenges

You don't have to live with the strain of social anxiety. You may always be a little nervous about certain social situations, but you should work to get yourself to the point that you don't completely avoid them. Challenge yourself to expand your boundaries and increase your comfort level in uncomfortable situations.

Check off once complete. Do as many or as few as you like. Make your own, based on the situations that make you anxious, focusing on the particular areas you want to improve.

- Present an idea at work that you are confident in that will be well-received.

- Present an idea at work that you are confident in, but is riskier in how it will be received.

- Start a conversation with a coworker you have only had brief interactions with.

- Make conversation with a stranger (in a safe, public setting).

- Take yourself out to lunch. Leave your phone in your pocket and your reading material at home.

- Show up to a dinner party by yourself.

- Join a book club.

- Start a book club.

- Ask your new neighbor to join you for a stroll around the neighborhood.

- Go for a walk by yourself and acknowledge the people you pass by. Keep your eyes off the ground.

- _____

- _____

- _____
- _____
- _____
- _____

Fear of Rejection

Most people fear rejection, but for an empath, this can be particularly poignant. Empaths are inherently loyal, caring, and generous, especially with the people they care about the most. As highly sensitive people, it is excruciating when they are shut out of someone's life or betrayed.

As empaths are often portrayed incorrectly in pop culture, they may be reluctant to "come out" to the people in their life. They worry that they will be viewed as weird and flaky or that they simply won't be believed. But you should feel free to tell people who you really are. Clarify what it means to be an empath. Make it clear that you do not view yourself as a supernatural being. Explain why certain people, places, and situations are stressful to you. This will help your loved ones to understand why you might tend to skip certain events or don't like to give long hugs. People that truly love you will continue to love and support you. They may never truly understand your gift, but give them a chance to accept it and accept you as you truly are.

Fear of Intimacy

While empaths fear rejection above all, they also fear to get too close to another person. They become overwhelmed with the aspect of dealing with the intensity of their own feelings, compounded with the strength of another person's feelings. As empaths enjoy having alone time, the prospect of the sensory overload from this much physical and emotional proximity can be very daunting. However, when you find the right partner, the relationship can empower you and help you feel more supported, connected, and grounded.

When you are entering into an intimate relationship, be open about who you are and what you need. Explain that you are an empath and what that means to you and the people in your life. This may not be a first date conversational topic, but don't wait too long. How the person reacts will be very telling. If someone misunderstands what an empath is, be understood of this and explain it to them. However, if you are mocked for being an empath, this is not someone you want in your life. Make sure that when you're in a relationship, you continue to focus on your self-care, as well as separating your emotions. You need someone who can handle when you need time alone.

Tips for Empaths in Intimate Relationships

1. Schedule some "me time" each day. This doesn't have to be a lot of time; you have a full schedule already! But you can spare five or ten minutes a day to take a walk, write in your journal, whatever you need to do to ground yourself and decompress. Once a week, schedule an hour to be alone and practice your self-care. Take a bath, meditate, do yoga, go for a hike, or spend time with your pet.

2. Be honest with your partner. If you need some extra time alone, be clear with them. If you had a day full of hand-shaking and meetings, you might need to sleep alone that night. Reassure your partner that it has nothing to do with them and you are just taking care of yourself. A worthy partner will respect that.

3. Ask your partner to be honest with you about their needs. If they are having a crisis and your partner needs you during your scheduled alone time, you don't want them to be afraid to tell you. When this happens, you can compromise. For example, you could give up your "me time" one day and take some extra time over the weekend. Or you could have a nice long talk, and then sleep separately.

4. If you cohabitate with your partner, have some physical space in your home that's just yours. Pop culture would refer to this as a "she-shed" or a "man-cave." But any space that is your own will do. Even if you share a bed on most nights, having your own bedroom you can retreat to can be helpful. If you live in a temperate climate, a garden, gazebo, patio, or porch might be right for you. Even a large closet that you convert into a reading nook

or meditation area could work. The most important thing is that you make it your own and you feel at ease when in the space. Unless there is an emergency, your pet should be the only visitor when you are in this space.

5. Remember, how you feel is just as important as how your partner feels. Don't be afraid to speak up. Don't be afraid to express an opinion that differs from his/her own. If you are an empath, one of your fears of being in an intimate relationship is likely that you will lose your sense of self to the other person. It is in your power to stop that from happening. Remember, your partner loves you for you. They want to be with you as you are, not simply an extension of them. If they want an extension of themselves, it may be time to consider finding a worthier partner.

Conquering fear of intimacy is important. Love is a crucial part of life, and with your gift, you can experience it even more strongly than most people. It is a lucky person who's loved by an empath. Be sure that in choosing a person to be in an intimate relationship with that you avoid Energy Vampires. As an empath, they will be drawn to you. See Chapter 5 for details.

Fear of Being Selfish

From a young age, we are taught that being selfish is bad. As people grow up, most of them forget this and become selfish. This is not the case for empaths. They continue to fear being selfish, even though they are the least likely people to be. It is important to remember there is a huge difference between being selfish and being someone who loves and takes care of himself/herself.

If you plant seeds but don't water them, you wouldn't expect to have flowers to pick. Likewise, you can't expect to be able to help others if you don't take care of yourself first. Taking care of yourself and making yourself a priority doesn't make you selfish. In fact, it will give you the energy to do more good in the world! You must learn balance. Determine how much time and energy you need to give to yourself so that when you help others, you can do so in a healthy, meaningful way.

The first step in overcoming any fear is to acknowledge it. Don't be ashamed of it. Fear is a natural reaction to danger. Humankind would be extinct by now if it weren't for fears. Don't ignore your fears; denial won't get you anywhere. Forgive yourself for having fears and those who have caused you to have fears. You may have developed a fear of rejection after being rejected; forgive the person who rejected you. There is no need to invite a toxic person who doesn't accept you for you back into your life. However, holding onto anger and resentment only does a disservice to you. It doesn't affect the person you are angry with. Forgiving allows you to let go, move on, and start conquering your fear. It gives you room in your life to let in positive emotions, good vibes, and people who are worth your time and energy.

Chapter 5:
Energy Vampires

"Self-absorption in all its forms kills empathy; let alone compassion. When we focus on ourselves, our world contracts as our problems and preoccupations loom large."

Daniel Goleman, Social Intelligence: The New Science of Human Relationships

Empaths are decadent feasts for energy vampires. Don't let them suck you dry and drain you of all your energy.

An energy vampire is someone who will suck out your positive emotions and drain your energy. It is someone who feels better by making those around them feel worse. Energy vampires are toxic people, especially to empaths. They make those around them feel anxious, depressed, hurt, and exhausted. This reaction is amplified when experienced by empaths. People with Narcissistic Personality Disorder and psychopaths are extreme species of energy vampires. The majority of energy vampires that you'll encounter are simply self-absorbed people with narcissistic tendencies. They may have positive traits as well, allowing them to disguise their metaphoric fangs.

It is important to point out the difference between energy vampires draining energy and empaths absorbing energy. Energy vampires feed on positive energy and give back nothing except negativity. Energy vampires also thrive on negative energy as it compounds with their own. When empaths absorb the positive energy of others, it does not deplete the other person because the empath is also emitting positive energy back to them. When an empath absorbs a person's negative energy, they are actually making that person feel better as they are taking away the negative and giving the positive.

Energy vampires are drawn to empaths by their compassion, altruism, and positive energy. Empaths have difficulty saying no and will continue to allow an energy vampire to feed upon them. The energy vampire will suck up all of that energy for them, leaving you feeling as drained and depleted as if you've been visited nightly by Dracula himself.

Is an Energy Vampire Preying on You?

Reading this, you probably have someone in mind that you suspect is an energy vampire. Unlike their bloodsucking counterparts, energy vampires can't be identified by an aversion to garlic and daylight, but you still recognize them. Please check off the statements that apply to your interactions with your suspected energy vampire. For this exercise, we will identify them as "Person V."

- When I am around Person V, I feel so lethargic. I have trouble being productive. I just want to sit around and do nothing.
- The ill effects of being around Person V last after I am no longer near to them. Our interactions keep negatively running through my mind, causing anxiety. Sometimes, it's more than anxiety. I feel bad about myself.

- After being away from Person V for about a week, I feel so much better! The venom has left my system. I feel re energized and productive, and I'm doing much better with maintaining my self-care!

- When I'm around Person V, I find myself taking on some of their traits, and I don't like or understand it! Why did I make that snarky comment about that woman's outfit? Why was I unsportsmanlike in that game of pick-up basketball?

- I am always there for Person V when they need me, but Person V never reciprocates this for me! I don't understand how they always expect me to drop everything for them, but never compromise when I am in need.

- I cannot reason or argue with Person V. They twist my statements and confuse me. I usually just give up and agree with them.

- Person V seems happy when things go wrong in my life.

- When good things happen in my life, Person V always finds a way to make me feel bad about myself.

- I suspect that Person V might have actively sabotaged me at some point.

If you have checked even one of these boxes, you have an energy vampire in your life. How many you check indicates how strong the energy vampire is. If you have checked all the boxes, it is time to sharpen your wooden stake metaphorically.

Classifying the Species of Energy Vampires

Narcissist Vampires

A *Narcissist Vampire* is someone who always puts themselves in the front and center of any situation. They manage to steer every conversation back around to their favorite topic—themselves. This is the type of person who will call you under the guise of wanting to see how you are. The conversation about you will be over in less than a minute. The remainder of the conversation will be about them. Did you break up with your significant other? Expect to hear about every breakup Narcissist Vampire has ever had. Your eighth-grader made the Honor Roll? You'll hear how Narcissist Vampire's child is on the fast track to the Ivy League. Is their child only in kindergarten? This doesn't matter to the Narcissist Vampire. It is always all about them, and they *always* have to be better. Narcissist Vampires excel and one-upmanship.

Narcissist Vampires range from the simply self-absorbed to a person who actually has Narcissistic Personality Disorder. They all lack empathy on a varying scale. This is arguably the most common species of an energy vampire. If the Narcissist Vampire is in your personal life, limit how much time you spend with them and the energy you expend on them. When you are on the phone with them, they are probably doing most of the talking anyway. You can multitask: clean, go for a walk, play with your pet, do some paperwork. Give them a couple of positive affirmations, and they will be happy.

A Narcissist Vampire at work can be a little trickier. The best way to deal with a Narcissist Vampire is to give them positive reinforcement, so they feel good about themselves and don't need to brag as much. However, you have to be more careful in the workplace. If you are working on a project and you have a great idea, they may (consciously or subconsciously) try to take credit for it. Don't let them. But when they have a great idea, praise them for it. If your superior at work is a Narcissistic Vampire, frame any requests you may have in ways that show how your request would be to their advantage. For example, if you need some time off, don't say that you are burnt out and need some time off. Frame the request so that you are asking for some time off because you don't feel you are operating at your best, and that you will be more productive when you return to the office. Being more productive will make your boss look better!

Narcissist Vampires and empaths are often drawn to each other. Like the old adage says: opposites attract. A narcissist can be quite intuitive and charming. They will know how to manipulate you and draw you in. Be careful! Do not enter in an intimate relationship with a Narcissistic Vampire. Because of their lack of empathy, they will never be able to understand you.

Victim Vampires

Victim Vampires love to be miserable and to spread misery. You had a bad day? They had a worse day. The most frustrating aspect of a Victim Vampire is that it is never their fault. The world has turned against them. They are a victim of their circumstances. They always ask for advice on how to fix their problems, but will rarely take it and often argue with you, telling you why it won't work. Victim Vampires will never run out of excuses.

Victim Vampires are exhausting and frustrating for everyone, not just empaths. But they are easy to deal with, as long as you maintain your boundaries. In personal life, limit the time you spend with them. They will try and drag you down. Be compassionate, but firm. Give them your full attention for a five-minute phone call. After the five minutes are up, say goodbye. Let them know they have your support, but you have to go. When you interact with a Victim Vampire in person, you can stick to the five-minute rule. Let them complain for five minutes. Be empathetic, but use your shield techniques to protect your emotions. Do not encourage their complaints. Once five minutes are up, change the subject. Don't back down if they resist. It may take several tries to make a successful subject change.

If the Victim Vampire is your coworker, limit personal conversations. Be kind, but keep your interactions professional. If they are complaining about your mutual boss, tell them you don't feel comfortable discussing it in the workplace. Tell them you think Person X might be able to hear the conversation. Whether or not Person X can actually hear the conversation is irrelevant. Be polite but firm. Use body language that lets them know you don't have time to wallow with them.

Rage Vampires

Rage Vampires are similar to Victim Vampires, in that nothing is ever their fault. However, unlike Victim Vampires, they go on the offensive and place blame on other people. A Victim Vampire will simply complain that they got a flat tire again and will claim that this is proof that the world is conspiring against them. A Rage Vampire will be accusatory and may claim something outlandish such as you noticed their tire was low and didn't tell them because you are trying to sabotage their chances at getting a promotion by making them late. Rage Vampires make empaths extremely uncomfortable. It is not only their emotions and energy that affect an empath, but also their tendency to yell, rant, and rave. This is overwhelming to their senses.

Do not engage with a Rage Vampire. Let them know that you hear them and you want to have a conversation with them, but set distinct boundaries. You will not continue the discussion until they have calmed down enough to stop yelling. If they won't stop yelling, disengage and walk away. If they cannot calm down enough to have a reasonable discussion, use technology as your fence. Email, text, or call. If you choose a phone call, turn down the volume on your phone. This puts you in control of the Rage Vampire's yelling.

Controlling Vampire

A *Controlling Vampire* will attempt to control how you're feeling and what you are doing. If they don't like how you are feeling, they will try to make you feel how they want you to feel or simply tell you how you feel. They will tell you what you need, what you want, and make you feel like a lesser person. You are NOT a lesser person. Controlling Vampires also have a tendency be overly critical.

Don't let a Controlling Vampire dominate your life. As with the Victim Vampire, be polite and firm. Thank them for their advice and concern, but assert that you will continue to do things your own way. If the Controlling Vampire is your superior in the workplace, it becomes tougher as they have the authority to tell you how to do your work. However, you can still find ways to be assertive. Don't let them talk down to you. If you have a better way to do something, explain it and respectfully let them know why you have chosen to do it that way.

When a Controlling Vampire is being critical of you, simply ask them to stop. Be firm and control your emotions as much as possible. Do not embrace the role of a victim. If they sense that you are getting emotional, they will feed off of this and will lead to more criticisms, such as "you're being too sensitive!"

Controlling Vampires in intimate relationships can be dangerous. If you feel that their controlling tendencies have gone too far or there is the potential for mental or physical abuse, get out safely. Let your friends and family know what's going on so they can be on alert and help you. Don't be afraid to call the police.

Drama Queen/King Vampire

The *Drama Queen/King Vampire* always must be the center of attention. A sneeze means they must have pneumonia! They had a great first date last night, and are now practically engaged!

Drama Queen/King Vampires can take almost any small incident and make into a huge deal. This is exhausting. Don't let yourself get caught up in the drama. Stay calm; the calmer you are, the less energy will be available for them to feed on. Here again, use your boundaries. With your personal life, set limits. With your co-workers, keep it polite and impersonal. "I'm so happy that you met 'the one' and are already planning your wedding after one date. But I'm sorry, I must get back to work. I have a deadline!"

Monologue Vampires

Monologue Vampires never stop talking. Empaths are wonderful listeners, and Monologue Vampires will suck up every ounce of listening energy that you have. They are not good at reading body language. They will not notice when you check your watch as a subtle message that you have to wrap up the conversation. They will not notice your crossed arms or attempts to insert yourself into the conversation. Since you don't have to participate in the conversation other than a few nods and "mmm hmm's," you'll have plenty of mental space to think of an excuse to end the conversation.

If you must continue to interact with the Monologue Vampire, be polite and firm. "Excuse me for interrupting, but I'd like to say…." A Monologue Vampire will not hesitate to interrupt you, so don't feel bad for interrupting them. You can use the technique of simply continuing what you are saying when a Monologue Vampire tries to interrupt you. You may have to raise your voice slightly to still be heard. This is uncomfortable for an empath, but the hope is that the Monologue Vampire will stop or at least pause when they notice that you are not backing down.

Staking Your Energy Vampire

You don't have to keep people in your life. In the case of an energy vampire, you should not keep them in your life. They are toxic and will just continue to bring you down and steal your energy. In mythology, vampirism can spread by the venom from a bite. Likewise, the negativity an energy vampire spreads can be contagious. If you have too much exposure to their negativity, they may even succeed in making you a negative person like them. With your gifts as an empath, that would be a shame for you, the people who love you, and the world at large. Don't let an energy vampire keep you from spreading your positive energy into the world.

The best way to stake an energy vampire is to simply cut them out of your life. Make a clean break and second-guess yourself. Realistically, it's not always possible to cut someone completely out of your life.

If Person V is only a low-level energy vampire who you value and has other redeeming qualities, you might choose to keep them in your life. It will be important for you to make your boundaries clear with this person. You might also choose to phase them out partially, so you are not as big parts of each other's lives.

An energy vampire may be toxic, but they aren't necessarily a bad person. They may simply be learned behavior from their childhood or a defense mechanism. You can talk to the person about how they are making you feel. They may have no idea that the way they are acting is hurtful and decide that they want to change! It's not recommended to actually use the term *energy vampire* when broaching this subject. Take a gentler approach. If the energy vampire is committed to making a change in their life, you can support them through this process. However, approach this with caution. The energy vampire may claim they want to change, but with no intention of doing so. They may be attempting to manipulate you into staying in their life and giving them even more attention and energy. Making changes will be their journey. You can offer them support and guidance, but don't let them make this into another opportunity to prey upon your emotions and energy. If you do not see them making positive changes, you may have to cut them out of your life.

Person V might be a family member. It is extremely hard to cut a family member out of your life. Start by talking to them. If they are unwilling to make any changes, you can choose to make them a less prominent part of your life. If someone, even a family member, is making you truly unhappy, it may be best to truly cut ties. It is not a choice to be made lightly, but you have to do what is truly right for you, your health and happiness, and your life.

To counteract the energy vampires in your life, try to surround yourself with people who are kind, loving, and who reciprocate your generosity and nurturing nature. These are the people that you want to absorb energy from, and in return, share energy and time with.

Antidotes for the Bite of an Energy Vampire

As you are encouraged to not isolate yourself, it is inevitable that you will encounter energy vampires. The toxic energy and negative emotions will last after you are no longer in their presence. You may feel physically exhausted and experience brain fog. Self-care practices mentioned in Chapter 2 such as meditation, yoga, exercise, and a hot Epsom salt bath will you clear your mind and rejuvenate your body.

Try taking a hot shower. As you scrub, visualize cleaning and rinsing away the lingering toxic energy. Use products with a calming scent such as ginger or lavender, or simply a scent that makes you feel happy and clean.
Try aromatherapy. Scents such as lavender, sage, eucalyptus, and spearmint are very helpful in relaxing and clearing the mind. Before using essential oils, do your research. Most are too potent to be applied directly to the skin and benefit from being mixed with a gentle carrier oil. If you use a diffuser and have a pet, make sure that the essential oil you are diffusing is non-toxic to your animal. Most essential oils should also be diluted when they are diffused. The smaller your space, the more careful you need to be.

Talk to a friend. You may not have any empaths in your life, but hopefully, you have empathetic people that you are close <u>to</u>. You always support others; it's <u>fine</u> to ask for support once in a while. People that frequently lean on you will be pleased that you are finally leaning on them! Spending time with a positive person will help you feel better by absorbing their energy. It will also help to remind you that there are other kind, giving people in the world. Not everyone is an energy vampire.

Chapter 6:
Developing Your Skills

"Sow a thought, and you reap an act; sow an act, and you reap a habit; sow a habit, and you reap a character; sow a character, and you reap a destiny."

Charles Reade (1814-1884)

Until now, we have taken a straightforward, practical approach. We have reached the point at which you must open your mind and broaden your horizons. Take a risk and consider that not everything in life is linear. There are some things in life that we may never fully understand. Keep in mind that while being an empath is super, it's not a superpower. You are a normal person with a gift. You are not a character out of science fiction. What you experience might not be average, but this does not make you abnormal.

The first step in developing your skill as an empath is to try to determine what kind you are. Keep in mind that these are neither guidelines nor boundaries. You might fit quite neatly into a category, or you might have a little bit of each.

Types of Empaths

The most common type is the *Emotional Empath*. This type of empath is the closest to the simple definition as someone who feels the emotions of others as their own. Most empaths will have some degree of this ability.

A *Physical Empath* or *Medical Empath* feels the energy of others. They can intuit what is wrong with someone. These types of empaths are often drawn to healing career fields, whether it be traditional medicine or alternative medicine, such as acupuncture. Some physical or medical empaths can sense blockages within a person's energy field. Those that focus and work to develop their abilities may even succeed in unblocking energy fields.

A difficulty that physical or medical empaths can face is that they may actually be able to feel the physical symptoms of others in their own bodies. For those that work in healing, this can be very useful in diagnosing the issue. It is very important that they learn to control this ability so that they can function in their daily work.

Geomantic Empaths are incredibly tuned into their physical surroundings. They may feel an unexplained connection to certain places or extreme dread at others. They can pick up on places that have borne witness to intense emotions. A geomantic empath would have a strong reaction to places such as historical battlefields.

Geomantic empaths are highly attuned to the environment. Many nature lovers would be devastated to see an area of deforestation, but geomantic empaths would experience a particularly poignant sense of pain and loss. Although all empaths are drawn to nature and benefit from spending time in it, for a geomantic empath, this is even more essential. If you are a geomantic empath and don't live in an area where you can easily access nature, bring it into your home. Potted plants, natural wood furniture, linen and cotton materials, and a pet would all be beneficial for maintaining positive energy and a grounded sense of self.

Plant Empaths are like physical empaths for plants. When they see plants, they instinctively know what they need. If you are a plant empath, you are probably known for having a "green thumb." Some plant empaths actually feel the energy that plants give off. Others claim to be able to hear what plants are telling them and receive guidance from them. Like geomantic empaths, they will feel healthier and happier if they are frequently able to spend time in nature. They will also benefit from bringing potted plants into their living areas. They may bond with certain plants more than others.

Animal Empaths can feel the emotions of animals. Many animal empaths can also sense what animals need or if they are ill. Most find some way to work with animals, whether as their career or volunteering. Some of them claim to be able to communicate telepathically with animals. If you have an animal empath in your life, be prepared to be surrounded by feathers, fur, scales, and the happiest, healthiest animals you'd ever want to see!

Claircognizant or *Intuitive* Empaths can receive information from people, just by being around them. Back in Chapter 1, we used the example of a student who knows the answers to a test but didn't study. This would be an example of a claircognizant or intuitive empath. However, if you know a school-age claircognizant, remind them that they still need to study; their gift won't always get them good grades, and they can pick up on the wrong answers some of their classmates may have! This is the type of empath who would intuit if someone was lying, whereas an emotional empath would pick up on how the emotions experienced while the lie was being told.

It may be difficult to believe that some empaths can communicate with plants or animals. It is up to you to decide what you believe in. Keep in mind that, although telepathic communication with plants and animals cannot be scientifically proven, it cannot be scientifically disproven either. If you find yourself meeting a plant empath, ask to see their garden. If you come across an animal empath, ask them to meet your pet. It might just open your mind to the possibilities.

Finding a Mentor

The internet and social media have a lot of drawbacks. However, it can help you to find other empaths that you can share your experiences with. Typing "empath + blog" into a search engine will yield over 6 million results. This is a great place to start looking into the empath community, especially if you are shy and would prefer to remain anonymous.

Be confident in yourself. You have a rare and beautiful gift. Tell people you are an empath; you might find that they are one too or they might know one they can introduce you to. Is there someone that you particularly admire because they are so kind and always seem to make the people around them feel better? Ask them if they are an empath. If they aren't, then no harm done—you have simply given them a lovely compliment.

Once you have found a mentor, even if they are a different classification of empath as you, you'll have someone who truly understands your experiences and who can advise you on how to control and develop your abilities.

Practice Visualization

We briefly discussed practicing visualization to help with social anxiety in <u>Chapter 4</u>, but we will take a different approach here. Part of developing your gifts as an empath is learning to control them. This will allow you to better handle people, situations, and places that would otherwise take a toll on your emotions and make you feel drained. When you practice visualization, do so for at least 5 minutes. Turn off any electronics that you can, quiet your environment, and get into a comfortable position. When the preparations are complete, the first step to any visualization technique discussed here is to clear your mind and concentrate on your breathing. The final step will be to bring yourself back to consciousness slowly.

Grounding Visualization

When you are feeling overwhelmed, or before an event you know will result in sensory overload, practice grounding visualization. If you can do this outside, it will be even more centering. Picture yourself as a tree. Beneath you, roots are growing from your feet, deep into the earth, holding you steady. Use your roots to absorb the positive energy of the earth into yourself, causing you to grow and flourish. You are sprouting new, healthy, green leaves. Perhaps, you are a flowering tree. The buds are slowly opening, soaking in the sunshine. When you feel adrift in life, use this technique to feel grounded.

Shielding Visualization

Picture a field of energy around yourself. Consider it your aura if that imagery resonates with you. Give your field of energy characteristics that you feel are innate to you. Maybe it is a bright light, blue water, or a plant-like substance. Watch it billow and reach out to other people, giving them positive energy, and absorbing their energy. Now, pull the field of energy back towards yourself. Make it hug every curve. This is your shield. It has residue on it from the people it has come into contact with while reaching out to others. Shake your shield to wash away the residual energy and emotions of others. Now that it's clean, your shield is once again beautiful and lightweight. It will protect you from carrying the burden of others and keep your energy in and the emotions and energy of others out.

Bond-Cutting Visualization

You can use visualization to help cut out the energy vampires in your life. It can be difficult to lose a person, even if you know that it would be beneficial to both of you. Although you can tailor this technique to whatever works for you, start by visualizing yourself and Person V. There is a rope tying the two of you together. Think about your time together. Remember and forgive the bad. Remember and honor the good. Visualize yourself cutting yourself free from the bonds. Perhaps, you are cutting all the bonds if the person is particularly toxic. Perhaps, you are just fraying the bonds because you are choosing to keep them in your life as long as they respect your boundaries.

Protective Animal Visualization

If you are a Harry Potter fan, you may be familiar with the Patronus spell. This spell is cast as protection against Dementors, creatures that suck out happiness and eventually your soul. Dementors bear a striking similarity to energy vampires. When the Patronus spell is cast, the caster feels a connection with an animal which appears and fights off the Dementor. Likewise, try visualizing an animal that you feel a connection with. Picture it fighting off the energy vampires in your life, protecting you from them. It can be obviously a fierce animal, like a lion. However, it is more important that you feel a connection with the animal. Remember, even a domesticated house cat has claws and will use them. If you are an animal empath, the visualization of protective spirit animal may resonate with you more strongly than a shield.

Radio Visualization

While visualization is very helpful with establishing boundaries, it can also be used to help tune yourself into your empath abilities. Picture a radio, but instead of AM and FM, the frequencies are your emotions and other people's emotions. Picture yourself turning on the radio. Tune into your emotions and turn the volume up. With this picture in your mind, use the skills you have developed while practicing separation to concentrate on the emotions you are experiencing. When you are ready, slowly turn down the volume and tune to other people's emotions. Slowly turn the volume up and focus on feeling the emotions of people around you. Finish my tuning down the emotions of others and tuning back to your own. You can use this visualization technique when you are working on separating your emotions from others, as well as when you are trying to focus on other people. For people in an intimate relationship, this type of boundary visualization may feel less harsh than the shield or protective animal.

Keep practicing your visualizations. Modify them, so they work for you and feel natural. Don't be discouraged if it takes time. Be confident that you will eventually get to the point when you can visualize your shield, cutting bonds, or your guardian animal, and be able to keep your energy in and other energy out. However, the visualization is not a miracle worker. If you spend too much time with a particularly venomous energy vampire, they will still manage to drain you.

Meditate Daily

The goal of this book is to encourage you to embrace your gift as an empath, while still living a normal life. Most people don't have much spare time. Your meditation can be part of your daily self-care routine. Although you should aim to practice daily, if you only have a few minutes, use the little time you have, instead of wasting time being anxious that you don't have more time to dedicate to the practice.

The goal of your meditation will be to clear your mind and will honor your body. Rid yourself of sensory overload. This will help you release the emotions of others, understand your own emotions, and focus. Meditation also increases the production of endorphins in your body, as well as decreases your levels of cortisol.[3]

Take a class, use an app, do a guided video on YouTube. There are many free options available. It takes practice to feel the long-term effects of meditation. Be patient with yourself. If you get frustrated, take the time to think of how you would react if a friend told you they were having trouble meditating. Would you tell them that they probably were not able to master it and that they should just give up? Or would you tell them that they should keep trying, they'll get the hang of it? The answer is clear. Empaths, please remember to be empathetic to yourselves!

Once you master clearing your mind through meditation, this can be a powerful tool that you can implement at any time. At work, take a five-minute break in your office or even in the restroom. In your personal life, excuse yourself to your personal space or take a walk. You can quickly shed the sensory overload and lessen how drained you feel.

When you meditate, the end goal is to have a clear mind. However, do not force yourself to empty your mind. Let your thoughts float by as you concentrate on slow, deep breathing. Wait for them to pass. Focus on each part of your body, one at a time. Start at your feet, move your way up. As you focus your awareness on each body part, honor what it does to support you. Are you a woman that wears high heels all day every day? Honor your feet for supporting you. Are you a man whose hands are toughened with calluses because you work with them every day? Honor your hands for providing your livelihood. If a part of your body is experiencing discomfort, focus on bringing your loving energy to that body part. Finally, focus on bringing awareness, healing, and love to your pineal gland or third eye.[4] It's up to you whether you are more comfortable viewing this particular area of the brain from a scientific or mystical perspective.

---

[3] Cortisol is commonly known as the stress hormone. It has many negative impacts on your body. Cortisol hinders memory and your ability to learn. It lowers your immunity, and increases your risk of experiencing depression.

[4] The third eye is mystical in origin, and has the sense of intuition.

As you conclude your meditation, thank your body; affirm that you are fully embracing your abilities as an empath. Finally, return to the present and slowly open your eyes.

Use Affirmations

You can use affirmations to accept yourself as an empath and strengthen your abilities. Choose empathic qualities that you particularly want to embrace and enhance. You can also pick qualities that you already have plenty of and use your affirmations to remind yourself of your value. It will be beneficial to you if you include an affirmation about maintaining boundaries.

Develop a routine. Schedule some time each day to practice your affirmations. This is different from meditation; you can multitask, as long as the tasks are mostly physical and you can apply your mental focus to the affirmations.

Use your affirmations. Don't just pick your affirmations randomly; take the time to write them down. It can be a valuable exercise to journal about your affirmations and why you picked each one. When you practice your affirmations, this can be done in your head spoken aloud, or you can even sing them. If you know sign language, you can sign them. Choose what feels best for you and is appropriate to the situation.

Associate your affirmations with your senses. This can be very helpful to empaths whose senses are stronger than the average person's is. You can use a different color pen to write down each of your affirmations. As you practice, you will start to associate the colors with the affirmations, even when you're not doing them. This will serve as an everyday reminder for you. A scent is another powerful tool you can use. That's because the olfactory bulb, a structure in the brain which controls our sense of smell, is a part of the limbic system, which is central to memory. Make your sense associations part of your daily affirmation practice.

Forgive, don't judge yourself. If you don't have time to do your affirmations for a day or even a week, don't criticize yourself. If you let negative thoughts enter while doing your affirmations, relax, dismiss them, and continue. If you have trouble getting into the habit, start slow.

To help you really enjoy all the positive benefits of affirmations, I have prepared a little gift for you. In chapter 9 of this book you'll find two guided meditation sessions that use affirmations to help you accept yourself as an empath and strengthen your positive abilities and qualities. I hope you'll like it!

Empaths and the Pineal Gland

The pineal gland, named for its pinecone-like shape, is a pea-sized gland in the brain located between the left and right hemispheres. This gland is our source of melatonin, a hormone that regulates circadian rhythm. [5] The pineal gland is located in the area of the brain where the conscious and subconscious brain meet. Activating the pineal gland allows us to expand our senses to access the subconscious level. Before science discovered the existence of the pineal gland, this area of the brain was known in mystical circles as a third eye. When this third eye was opened, it allowed the person to increase their levels of awareness, consciousness, and intuition.

The pineal gland is very important in being able to access your abilities as an empath. Diet, medicines, lifestyle, and lack of use can calcify the pineal gland. This disrupts your biorhythms and connection to your intuition.

Detoxifying the Pineal Gland

Detoxifying the pineal gland is an important part of embracing your empathic abilities, particularly in improving your sense of intuition.

Consider an organic, locally based, raw food diet to help decalcify your pineal gland. It is important to speak to your doctor prior to making drastic changes to your diet. Your health is more important than accessing

---

[5] Circadian rhythm is your body's internal clock. It regulates your schedule of sleep and wakefulness. It is what gets thrown off when daylight savings time begins and ends.

your abilities as an empath. Eating food that is alive, like fresh, locally grown fruit and vegetables, will provide you with energy and mental balance. Some empaths can see the different auras between foods that are alive and dead. Fresh, locally-sourced produce will have a different feel, look, taste, and energy than produce that has come from mass farms and transported long distances. Geomantic empaths will benefit the most from locally-sourced food; this is very grounding for them.

Cutting out meat can be particularly beneficial for animal empaths, who may feel the emotion and energy of animals they eat. If you choose to cut meat out of your life, it is very important to consume sufficient amounts of alternate sources of proteins and healthy fats. Plant and geomantic empaths can benefit from eating food so close to their natural form. Talk to your doctor before making major changes in your diet, such as eliminating meat or only eating raw foods.

Watch your fluoride intake. Sodium fluoride calcifies the pineal gland because it contains metals like aluminum and arsenic. It has some benefits; it is used in pharmaceuticals, medical imaging, and dental work, and also increases bone density. An excess of sodium fluoride in your body can cause many issues, such as overhardening of the bones and problems with the heart.

Sodium fluoride can be found in tap water, bottled spring water, toothpaste, deodorant, and processed foods. There are easy switches you can make to decrease your fluoride consumption. You can buy alkaline water or install a water filtration system, which would be a more ecologically friendly solution. When choosing a water filtration system, make sure that fluoride removal is specified. Most common household filters do not remove fluoride.

When you shop for toothpaste and deodorant, look for ones that do not contain fluoride. These can be found at health stores and often the natural sections of mainstream grocery stores.

Avoid using Teflon-coated cookware, as this can increase the fluoride content of the foods you are cooking.

When your doctor prescribes medicine, ask if it contains fluoride. If it does, they may be able to recommend a fluoride-free alternative that will be equally effective. Prior to going into surgery, inquire about using an anesthetic that doesn't contain fluoride. If your doctor tells you that you need a medicine, even though it contains fluoride, listen to your doctor. Explain your concerns about physical problems fluoride can cause. Your doctor will be more concerned about your physical well-being than awakening your latent empathic abilities. Feel free to get a second or even third opinion, but your health should be your priority. If you are committed to decreasing your fluoride consumption, make up the difference in other ways.

Make your bedroom as dark as possible and get enough sleep. This darkness doesn't refer to your choices in decor. Try to eliminate all light sources when it's time to sleep. When you are in the dark, you produce more melatonin. This activates the pineal gland and helps you to sleep better, ensuring a healthy circadian rhythm. Turn off all the lights, TV, computer, tablets, and phones. If you must have your cell phone in the bedroom, put it in a drawer. Consider investing in blackout curtains. Try to get a full eight-hour sleep each night. Try to maintain a routine of going to bed and waking up at the same time each day.

Gaze at the sun without sunglasses. Do this safely and comfortably. If you are going to look directly at the sun, do so early in the morning. This stimulates the pineal gland through its photoreceptors. If you watch the sunrise regularly, this is beneficial to your biorhythm. It communicates to your mind and body that it's time to be awake and active.

Practice yoga. Yoga, practiced mindfully with a focus on breathing, connects the mind and the body and stimulates the pineal gland. It is also very relaxing and good for your body.

Turn off technology! Today's lifestyle is not conducive to completely shunning technology. In some ways, technology can be very beneficial to empaths. However, limiting technology use, especially before you go to bed, can be very helpful. Cell phones and computers produce low levels of radiation, which stunts the pineal gland's growth and melatonin production. Blue light, which is emitted by cell phones, tablets, and computers, disrupts your sleep by interfering with your circadian rhythm. Try to turn your electronics off 15 minutes before you go to bed. Gradually work your way up to an hour. Don't just put your computer on sleep mode, actually turn it off. When you turn off the mind-numbing drone of social media, you can be more mindful. You can't meditate while checking your Facebook feed!

Embrace Spirituality

Most people think that mystical religions go hand-in-hand with empaths. Although they certainly can, embracing spirituality through any source will help you envelop your life in peace and protection. Catholics can be empaths as easily as Buddhists. Even atheists can experience a form of spirituality. You may not believe in a higher power, but instead, you feel spiritually in tune with nature. Embracing spirituality in life and the interconnectedness of the world will help you to access your intuition. If you are battling with addiction from trying to numb yourself against sensory overload, embracing your spirituality will help you. Spirituality is an integral part of the Twelve-Step Program. In the case of spirituality, the importance is not getting answers; it is asking the questions and taking the journey of seeking answers. You cannot reach the point of having a complete spirituality. As you develop your spirituality, you will continually uncover more mysteries within yourself and the universe to investigate.

Embracing spirituality will help you to accept your empath skills with the knowledge that you're not challenged by what you are equipped to handle. What you can handle will continually change throughout your lifetime. Whether your belief system centers around God, Goddess, gods and goddesses, Buddha, Mother Nature, or simply an unnamed Higher Power, you will find that this is a central tenet. You can face whatever you are challenged with. It is up to you to do your best and awaken your latent abilities.

The Journey of Enhancing and Developing Your Empath Skills

You won't develop your empath skills overnight. It is a journey of self-discovery and an exploration of your senses that stretch beyond you as an individual. You will examine the interconnectivity of the world: its people, animals, plants, and the environment as a whole.

Stage 1: Burdened with the Weight of the World

You haven't accepted your gift of empathic skills yet, and you try to numb your sensitivities. You may be isolating yourself or relying on alcohol and drugs to get you through social situations. You wish you were less sensitive and more like the average person. You may not yet know what empaths are and you have a negative outlook on your future.

The good news is, if you are reading this book, you are already transitioning out of this phase. You are accepting that you're different from other people, and that's not a bad thing. Hopefully, you are coming to realize that, while being an empath is not easy, it is also not a curse. You are ready to learn more about yourself and your skills.

Stage 2: Embracing Self-Care

You have accepted that you are special and have begun to shift your self-paradigm so that you are no longer viewing yourself as a victim of your abilities. You are focusing positively on taking care of yourself rather than wallowing in your difficulties. Instead of trying to numb yourself so that you can function in large groups, you are taking the time to yourself to be alone, to reflect, and to decompress.

Stage 3: Research and Experimentation

You've been focusing on yourself, but now you are ready to get back into the world! This is a very important phase and one that readers of this book are most likely in. You have accepted that you have a strong sense of other people's emotions and energy and have begun to do your research to figure out how and why. At this point, you have probably classified yourself as an empath. You are getting comfortable with meditating and have begun practicing visualization.

Stage 4: Training

You are getting excited about your abilities and starting to try to enhance them. You're becoming more skilled at shielding and finding yourself better at functioning in group settings. You have realized that, while your empathic skills may not be fully developed yet, they are your strength and it can help you to do some good in the world. You feel that you have gained some control over your destiny. You have accepted that you might not always feel comfortable, but are becoming more adept in handling the discomfort. You are utilizing healthy methods to decompress and recover after overwhelming situations. You may have found a training program to attend or you are practicing using books and online resources. You are on the lookout for other empaths, whether they be in your personal life or an online community.

Stage 5: Skill Management

You've reached the point where you have better control over your skills. You're learning to apply and control them with more ease and less conscious effort. You are feeling decreased guilt when asserting your boundaries or even cutting energy vampires completely out of your life. You feel more centered and in control of the direction your life is taking.

Stage 6: Emotional Clarity

You can now be in crowds and not feel overwhelmed. Without much effort, you can separate your emotions from the emotions you experience through others. You are aware of the energy that surrounds you, but you don't absorb it unless you invite it in. Your skills are not perfect. You remember the importance of practicing self-care and don't feel guilty about making this a priority. When you are feeling run down, you may still be vulnerable to the emotions and energies of the people you are near. However, it is now easier for you to recover. You can access and, more importantly, to trust your intuition.

Stage 7: Life Goes On

You may choose to employ your empathic abilities every day. You may forget for days or even weeks that you have them. It's your choice whether you want to use your skills or to simply control them. If you choose just to control them, there may be a time when you don't even think about being an empath. You are subconsciously using the shielding and separation skills you've been developing. Don't be discouraged if you have days when you are overwhelmed by emotion or depleted of energy. Remember, this is a skill that is super, not a superpower. When you are using your talents to help others, it's not with a sense of guilt or burden. It is because you truly want to spread love and positive energy in the world.

Chapter 7:
Wielding Your Gift

"It is one of the beautiful compensations of life that no man can sincerely try to help another without helping himself."

Ralph Waldo Emerson (1803-1882)

Now that you have developed and learned to control your gifts, it's time to use them!

Strategize

You have the unique ability to sense energy and emotions that others do not. There is nothing wrong with using this to your own benefit. People use more obvious talents, looks, intelligence, and confidence to get ahead in life. You are simply using a talent and quality that is rarer.

If you are in a client meeting, focus on the client. You'll be the first among your co-workers that can tell if the client doesn't like the direction that the presentation is headed in. Use your skills to hone in on what the client wants and modify the ideas you are presenting accordingly.

Stop Problems While They Are Still Small

You can pick up on energies and emotions that will tell you when there is a problem brewing in your life. Face the problems before they get too big to handle.

At work, can you feel the tension building between two co-workers? Meet with them and see if it can be resolved. Depending on your field, you may not feel comfortable sharing with your co-workers that you're an empath; this is fine. It's a good idea to keep your personal life separate from work. You can frame the conversation as just checking in. You may be able to point out an incident that clued you in without mentioning your empathic abilities. You can tell them that you have noticed tension; they won't jump to the conclusion that you are an empath.

In your personal life, is there a resentment building between two of your friends? Schedule a meal with them both, during which you can all talk about how you are feeling. In this setting, it is more appropriate to mention that you sensed this using your abilities as an empath.

Improve Your Personal Relationships

With your friends, family, and in intimate relationships, you will be able to sense the people's needs and wants, perhaps before they even realize it themselves. You will be able to tell when they want to talk and need support, and conversely when they need space. Empaths love to fix things, but often people don't want advice; they want to be heard and supported. If you focus on your intuitive senses, you will be able to tell when to give advice and when to simply listen. When it is appropriate for you to give advice, you can uniquely give great advice! Listen to your intuition; it will set you on the right path.

Improve Your Work

You can tell when your boss is in a bad mood or when he/she is feeling particularly generous. Time yourself accordingly. If you have good news, share it with your boss when he/she is in a bad mood. This will help you develop a positive reputation as someone who makes things better. Wait until your boss is feeling generous, and then ask for a raise. Remember, you're not taking advantage of anyone. Everyone has talents they use in the workplace. Intuition is simply one of your talents.

Can you tell that the person in the position you want is starting to look at other companies? Start focusing your energy on demonstrating that you would be perfect for that position. When the job opens up, you will be several steps ahead in proving you're the right person to take their place.

Tap into your intuition to solve problems, know what direction you should take your projects and how to interact with people. When meeting a potential client, focus on intuiting how they like to be wooed. Are they someone who like to get to know someone they are doing business with? Suggest a business lunch or dinner and be open with them, while remaining professional. Perhaps, you can sense that the potential client likes to compartmentalize. Work is work; it has no place for the personal. In this case, forgo the lunch meetings. Keep the small talk mundane and impersonal. Mention the weather, but don't ask if they have any exciting plans for the weekend. This doesn't mean that you have to be unfriendly, just keep the discussions focused on business.

Brace Yourself

You can tell when something big is about to happen. Is your significant other acting oddly? Focus on their energy and emotions. They could be planning to propose or they could be considering ending the relationship. Maybe they are up for a promotion at work but would have to move. They may be concerned that you won't want to come with them. Perhaps, they're looking outside the relationship for physical intimacy. Focus and listen on your intuition, even if you don't like what it is telling you. This can help you decide how you'll handle changes and if it's worth remaining in the relationship. Before making any major, life-altering decisions, talk to your partner. You may be misinterpreting what you are intuiting.

Are you sensing major changes ahead in your place of work? If you intuit that the company is not doing well, you can get ahead of any potential layoffs by starting to search for a position in another company. Sensing positive changes and growth? Work to position yourself so that you will be a part of the positive change, ideally with a promotion and raise!

Help Someone

If someone tells you that they have considered harming themselves or others, do not rely on your empathic abilities to help them. If this happens at work, report it. If it happens in your personal life, report it. Encourage the person to seek help from a trained medical professional. The support you provide can only be secondary. If someone has gotten to that point, your gift is not enough to save them or others no matter how developed your abilities are.

Aside from this warning, we will not examine how to help someone with serious depression. In these cases, you can use the strategies below, but that will only be supplemental to treatment by a trained medical professional. Don't tell anyone to go against the advice of a trained medical professional. If you don't agree with anti-anxiety medications, keep that opinion to yourself. If you are truly concerned that someone has not received proper care, advise them to get a second opinion from another doctor. Unless you are a trained medical professional, the second opinion shouldn't be your opinion. If you suspect neglect or abuse in care facilities, report it.

If your senses tell you that someone is going through a hard time and wants to ask for help but doesn't know how, reach out to them. You don't have to tell them that you could sense this, just be your normal, kind, supportive self and talk to them. Ask them about their lives. Sometimes, people just need to feel like someone cares to feel better.

If you are a physical empath, you may sense someone is ill. Encourage them to see a trained medical professional for treatment. If you can sense they are afraid to go alone, offer to go with them if this would be appropriate. Particularly with co-workers, it may not be proper for you to go to certain appointments with them, but you could make suggestions. You could also offer to drop them off or pick them up and entertain yourself nearby during their appointment.

Can you tell that someone in your life is simply struggling with overwork, and doesn't have time to take care of themselves? If you have the time, help them out. If your friend just had a baby, stop by and do a load of dishes and laundry. If your coworker has too much on their plate, and you don't have enough, talk to them to see if they can delegate anything to you. Is your partner working late every night? Have a nice dinner waiting for them at the end of the day. Mentally prepare yourself not to be angry if they are late! This is counterproductive. Choose a meal that can handle holding heat for an extended period of time. Encourage your partner to take a nice relaxing bath while you clean up.

In Chapter 2 we discussed doing good in the world by volunteering. Now that we have learned about the different types of empaths, we will discuss ideas that would suit each type's talents. Remember, although volunteering is a wonderful thing, and you'll be happy knowing you are helping others, you will bear witness to depressing situations as well as people, animals, and plants that are in pain. Make sure you increase your self-care before and take the time to decompress after. You are not being selfish. This self-care will help you to continue helping others.

Crisis Hotlines

In these types of organizations, people call in when they feel they don't have anyone in their lives that they can go to. Emotional and Claircognizant/Intuitive empaths are excellent in this type of service. Emotional empaths can pick up emotions. Since it is through the phone, it is not as draining for them as it would be in person. Claircognizant/Intuitive empaths can intuit the type of advice that would best help this person and to sense if he/she requires more help than talking on the phone can give. Please rely first and foremost on the training you will receive and use your empathic abilities as a supplement. For example, if a person is using language that would normally trigger a reaction of sending help to them, but you sense they do not need additional help, abide by your training and call for help. You could be picking up on the emotions of someone else nearby. Do not risk anyone's health, safety, or life by testing your abilities.

The Peace Corps

The Peace Corps has many different divisions. A physical/medical empath would be an excellent health volunteer. You would participate in activities such as promoting basic hygiene, water sanitation, nutrition, maternal health, and child care. You could also work in the HIV/AIDS education and prevention programs.

Geomantic and plant empaths could find fulfillment in volunteering with the environmental and agricultural divisions. You would help spread knowledge of environmental issues and teach communities to use their natural resources sustainably. You would also help instruct farmers on how to implement techniques that will provide a bountiful harvest without the use of dangerous chemicals and pesticides.

Fostering Animals

There are so many abused, neglected, and homeless pets in the world. An animal empath would be a wonderful foster pet parent, particularly for animals that have been abused and neglected. An animal empath will be able to calm and nurture an animal that has issues with trust and is scared of affection in ways that an average person wouldn't understand or have the capability to do. They will instinctively know when the animal needs space. If an animal is showing signs of aggression, but you are not picking up on the aggression in their energy fields, still use caution. Your pineal gland may be blocked, and you could be missing signals. Do not endanger yourself.

Finding Fulfillment in Your Career

"Have the courage to follow your heart and intuition. They somehow already know what you truly want to become."

Steve Jobs (1955-2011)

If you're an empath that finds fulfillment in a traditional, corporate-type job, that's great! However, most empaths feel more comfortable in jobs that embrace their creative nature and their desire to help others. If you find that you are drained, unhappy, and uninspired by your career, it's never too late to make a change. The wrong job can make you feel like you are surrounded by especially venomous energy vampires that you are unable to stake. We're not advocating quitting your job. We are simply suggesting that you evaluate your current position and if it makes you happy and inspires you. You may decide to change fields. You may decide that you are willing to put up with a job you don't feel passionate about because of the financial security it provides. You can find passion and fulfillment elsewhere. The important thing is to be aware and embrace that your life is not predestined. You make the choices that affect your destiny. You are in charge of your own life. Live it well.

What is Meaningful to You?

"Let the beauty we love be what we do. There are hundreds of ways to kneel and kiss the ground."

Jalal al-Din Rumi (1207-1273), translated by Coleman Barks

Empaths feel most fulfilled in career paths that are meaningful to them and allows them to employ their specific gifts. Don't worry about what you think other people will consider meaningful. Your opinion is what matters. You may find fulfillment while working with children with special needs. You might find it in making people feel confident and beautiful. Whether you become a special education teacher or esthetician, you are making an impact on people's lives and how they feel about themselves.

Plant and geomantic empaths may find fulfillment in the fields of landscaping or gardening, specializing in native plants. You get to work with plants, help the environment, and make a beautiful, peaceful outdoor living space for people. Plant empaths would also make wonderful florists. Your working environment would surround you with positive energy and you would get to make people happy by providing beautiful goods.

If you find meaning in nurturing others, you may decide that working at a daycare or a long-term nursing facility is right for you. If this type of working environment would be too overwhelming to your senses, but you love to cook and bake, consider opening a bakery or starting a catering company. You would be providing a good that nurtures people's mind and bodies.

Empaths of all types can make great health care professionals, particularly therapists, psychologists, and psychiatrists. If you choose this field, separation and shielding will be integral to your daily life. You may have to adjust your appointment schedule so that you have a few minutes to decompress after seeing exceptionally difficult patients, especially if they happen to be energy vampires. Physical empaths would excel in fields such as massage therapy or physical therapy.

There are fields that empaths typically do not thrive in. Sales or anything involving cold calling is often an empath's worst nightmare. This goes against their tendency to be introverts. It can be very painful for an empath to deal in sales, as they will be able to sense when they are annoying people. For salespeople to be successful, they have to be able to push through people's resistance. It is a career field best suited to extroverts. If you are an empath who enjoys your sales job, that's terrific! You likely have a highly-developed ability to shield and elevated levels of intuition, even for an empath.

Careers that involve arguing and promote aggressive behavior, such as a trial lawyer will not appeal to empaths. The courtroom drama will be constant sensory overload and will involve speaking and arguing in front of a crowd. This type of career goes against an empath's natural inclination to soothe and nurture.

Consider Your Co-workers' Energy

You might find a career that you find fulfilling, but hate the emotional energy that fills your workplace. This may have nothing to do with your chosen field, but a result of office politics, noise level, whether you have your own office, or a desk in a room with many of your co-workers.

It is not necessary to find a place of work that understands empaths, but you should find an environment that makes you feel comfortable, ideally with co-workers you can relate to on some level. No matter what field you find yourself in, no matter how philanthropic, you will encounter energy vampires. Avoid them politely.

Many empaths prefer fields that allow them to have a flexible schedule or work at home, such as artists or writers. With the development of technology, more fields can be welcoming to empaths. Perhaps, you are artistic and witty. Marketing or advertising might be a good fit for you. However, these types of fields are also attractive to energy vampires. Now, through the internet, emails, video conferencing, and text, an empath could do the work they enjoy from home and only come into the office for important presentations.

When you go in for an interview, spend as much time as you can meeting and simply being around your potential future co-workers. Let your shields down. Are the emotions you are experiencing more positive than negative? If they are negative, would you be able to work from home some days?

Consider the Workplace's Energy

When you walk into your workplace, tune into the energy. Does it feel positive or negative? If it is negative, can it be purified or easily improved? Are your senses soothed, stimulated, or overwhelmed? When you wake up in the morning, do you dread going to work, even though you find fulfillment in the job itself?

If you have the choice between two companies, with all other variables being equal, it will make sense to choose the company with physical energy you prefer. However, if you like your job or have a great opportunity, do what you can to improve the physical energy. Burning sage is a popular way to cleanse the energy of a physical space, but would not be a good idea to do in the workplace. Instead, you could spray rosewater, obtain permission to rearrange furniture and bring in a couple of plants or relaxing photos. Try to position your desk so that you are looking out a window. Turn off your computer when you are not using it. Try using noise-canceling headphones. Play music.

Chapter 8:
Loving an Empath

This final chapter is geared towards people who are not empaths, but whose loved ones are. You can use the information and advice given here to understand and support any empath in your life, but we will focus here on the most important members of your family: your child and life partner.

Raising an Empath

Raising a child is a rewarding and challenging journey. The goal of this section is not to tell how to raise your child. That is a very personal choice. We will simply aim to help you understand your child's unique needs as an empath and provide you tips to aid your child in embracing their gift. If your child turns out not to be an empath, nothing discussed here would be detrimental to implement.

Is My Child an Empath?

It will be hard to determine if your child is an empath or simply sensitive. Children tend to be more intuitive than adults. This is a talent that can fade as you age and experience self-doubt. Some clues will help you to figure out of your child is an empath. Trust your intuition as a parent. If you think your child is an empath, that is a huge sign. Please check off statements that you feel apply to you and your child.

- My child gets upset around crowds, loud noises, and stressful situations.

- My child knows things, and I can't figure out how he or she learned them!

- My child prefers his or her own company to that of other children.

- My child expresses frustration about not fitting in.

- My child can tell when I'm upset or stressed, no matter how hard I work to hide it from them.

- My child has one or two extremely close friends but doesn't have a large group of friends.

- My child doesn't like to go to have or go to parties, especially birthday parties.

- My child has always been a great listener and shows a great deal of compassion to other children, adults, and animals.

- I am frequently surprised by how strongly my child reacts to scary scenes in shows, movies, and books.

- During large family gatherings, my child tends to sneak off by his or herself.
- My child has an extremely strong bond with the family pet.

- My child seems most at peace in nature.

If you agree with zero of these statements, your child doesn't display the traits of an empath. Their talents lie elsewhere. Guide your child on the journey to find and embrace them. Get ready for a noisy home; you probably have an extrovert on your hands!

If you agree with 1-3 of these statements, your child is displaying some qualities of an empath.

If you agree with 4-6 of these statements, your child has moderate qualities of an empath.

If you agree with 7-9 of these statements, your child has high levels of qualities of an empath.

If you agree with 10-12 of these statements, congratulations, your child has exceptionally high levels of qualities of an empath.

Understanding and Supporting Your Empathic Child

Most parents emphasize being polite and present at family gatherings. If your child is an empath, being around a large group, with all the emotions a family brings out, can be very difficult. If the child tends to sneak away to be by themselves, they are not being rude and antisocial. It is simply too much for them. If they have grandparents that are hard of hearing, and most people are yelling to be heard, this is even worse; they are susceptible to excessive stimuli. They are also feeling the emotions of the family. For a child, it can be very scary and confusing to experience the emotions of adults. They don't understand why they are experiencing these emotions. In addition, they don't have the maturity and life experiences to understand the emotions they are feeling.

This sensitivity doesn't mean your child can't attend family gatherings and develop bonds with their extended family. The morning before the gathering, encourage your child to spend some time by themselves relaxing. You could suggest an activity like coloring, which along with being relaxing, is a mindful and creative outlet. This allows them to decompress so that when they enter into a situation that will overwhelm them, they are in a better frame of mind. If you can, bring along your pet. This companionship will help keep your child calm. If they are old enough, your child can take breaks from the family togetherness by taking their dog for a walk. Allow them to decompress again after the gathering. Encourage them to take a nice, warm bath. If they are young, supervise this like you would any bath, but forgo the bath toys. Keep the atmosphere serene.

Be understanding if your child doesn't often enjoy hugging or snuggling. Ask other family members and friends to be understanding about this too. Touch increases the absorption of energy so that excessive hugging can be very uncomfortable to empaths. Appreciate hugs when you get them, they will be even more special!

Encourage your child to keep a diary or journal. This will allow them to explore their feelings, instead of keeping them pent up. If your child doesn't understand how they are feeling, the act of writing about their confusion will help them to release these emotions. When they are old enough to understand, encourage them to use the method of journaling to practice the separation of other people's emotions from their own.

Keep screen time to a minimum. Even Disney movies can be sad and violent. I still can't watch *Bambi*! Encourage your child to read books instead. Although the storylines may be as sad and violent as movies, your child is at least avoiding the sensory stimuli from sound and flashing colors. Video games are loud, stressful on the eyes, violent, and can be addictive. Empaths are prone to addictive behaviors. Impose a strict time limit.

If your child prefers to have one or two close friends to a large group, respect that. During your school years, if you were an extrovert and had a large group of friends, you may wish for your child to have the same fun experience. Although this wish is made with great intentions, it's not necessarily right for your child. You may have loved going to big sporting events and parties. Understand that these may not be activities your child will enjoy. It will be overwhelming and highly uncomfortable to an empath. Encourage your child to have a healthy social life, but as they mature, don't try to shape it for them. Enjoy the time when they are young, and you have full control over playdates.

If your child is an empath, the school will be difficult for them. This doesn't refer to the academic aspects of the school. Your empathic child will likely be an excellent student, although reluctant to participate in class discussions. Schools are loud, often bright, and at least some areas will be smelly. This is not an easy environment for a child with heightened sensitivity to external stimuli. Compound this with all the emotions that they are experiencing through their schoolmates and teachers. When your child gets home, let them decompress and have some time alone before you ask them about their day. No matter how loving your intent and execution is, if you don't allow them to decompress first, they will feel bombarded.

You should do whatever you think is best for your child and their education, but there are options if you decide that your child's school is not a positive environment. If you choose to homeschool, there are standardized curriculums you can use. Online public schools are getting increasingly popular. There is also the more traditional route of the charter or private schools, which are usually less populated and often experience less violence than public schools. If you choose to keep your child in public school, that's fine! Not everyone has the time or funds to explore other options.
Respect your child's need for a private space. As a parent, you are interested in every aspect of your child's life. But it is very important that empaths have their own physical space to decompress. Help them to arrange their bedroom in a way that is peaceful to them. Get them a couple of plants to put in their room. Provide them with a sound machine or noise-canceling headphones.

Your empathic child might be very sensitive emotionally and to assaults on their senses, but they don't have a disability. Nor does this mean you can't correct their behavior, but have to give them free rein to run wild. They are still kids; they need structure and rules, and there should be consequences for breaking the rules. If your child breaks the rules, by all means, give them a lecture and punishment. During the lecture, try to be calm about it and attempt to avoid yelling. Be careful of how you discuss bad behavior. For example, statements such as "You were bad" should be replaced with "What you did was bad," followed by an explanation why. You may have to modify your paradigm for punishments. Being sent to their room to be alone would be a reward for an empath! Try assigning an undesirable chore instead.

All parents want to protect their children from the negative aspects of the world, particularly parents of empaths, who experience these negatives so strongly. But don't isolate your child. Negativity is inescapable, and they need to learn coping skills. You can't shelter your child forever. They need to develop boundaries and learn how to protect themselves.

Even Children Can Be Energy Vampires

If your child is an empath, energy vampires will be drawn to them. For the sake of this discussion, we will refer to suspected child energy vampires as "Child V." Please check off statements that you feel apply to your child and Child V.

- After spending time with Child V, my usually energetic and sweet-tempered child is exhausted, cranky, and tends to lash out.

- Child V has a negative effect on my child's self-esteem. I notice my child puts himself/herself down a lot more frequently after spending time with Child V.

- My child has confided to me that he/she is always there for Child V, but this is rarely reciprocated.

- When I witness the interactions between my child and Child V, Child V always makes it all about himself/herself and dominates the conversation.

- Whenever my child spends less time and energy with Child V, this results in Child V becoming increasingly clingy.

- I don't think that my child even likes Child V very much. He/she seems to maintain the friendship out of guilt.

If you have checked even one of these boxes, your child has an energy vampire in their life. How many you check indicates how strong the energy vampire is. Talk to your child. Let them know that it's perfectly fine to let go of a friend who doesn't treat them with kindness and compassion. Teach them by example. Have good friends yourself, let your child see how you treat each other.

Helping your child deal with energy vampires can be very tricky, especially as they get older. When your child is young, you can simply stop scheduling play dates for them with Child V. As they get older, especially into the preteen and teen years, telling your child not to be friends with Child V can backfire and they will likely hold even tighter to the friendship. Express your concerns, but as long as Child V is not putting your child in danger, there's not much you can do about the friendship. However, you can still help your child deal with this in a way they won't even realize. You are trying to raise your child to be a polite person, but after they spend time with Child V, give them a little grace if they are cranky and rude. Allow them to decompress.

Teach by Example

Throughout this book, we stress the importance of empaths practicing self-care. Practice self-care yourself, so your empathic child doesn't grow up thinking self-care is selfish. It will also help you! It is very important but is something that a lot of parents forgo, due to their busy lifestyle. Parents are very similar to empaths in this way. Parents forgo self-care to take care of their child. Empaths forgo self-care to take care of anyone they can. You can utilize the self-care practices discussed in Chapter 2, simply modify what you need and want to. Exercising, getting enough sleep, and taking a break from technology is good for anyone, not just empaths. If you take the time to reduce the stress, negative emotions, and negative energy in your life, your empathic child will also feel less stress and more positive emotions and energy.

Open Mind, Open Heart, Open Communication

As you learn more about empaths for the benefit of your child, you may discover you have some latent empathic abilities. Remember in Chapter 1, we learned that multiple empaths tend to be found in familial lines. Keep an open mind to the possibilities.

Children hate to be different from their peers. Talk to your child about empaths. It will be helpful for them to know that they are not the only ones experiencing emotions that aren't their own, and rushes or sudden depletion of energy. Start this at a young age and be positive about it, so that they grow up with the paradigm that being an empath is a good thing, not weird or a burden. However, you should acknowledge that it can be difficult, so they manage their expectations and realize that their frustrations with their ability are normal. Help your child practice visualization techniques discussed in Chapter 6. Modify the visualizations to their life. For example, you could lead them through the protective animal visualization, but have them use the family pet as their protective animal.

If your child has a bad feeling about someone, listen to your child. Don't let your child be alone with this individual. Do your best to cut this person out of your lives.

Make sure that your child knows you will always be there to support them. Encourage them to tell you about their empathic experiences. Ask them questions. Let them know that even if you don't fully understand their abilities, you believe in them and accept them. Be supportive of their goals. Communicate to them that you truly believe they can reach their goals and make a difference in the world.

Accept Yourself

You're a human and a parent, and you will make mistakes. If you get too angry and yell at your empathic child, forgive yourself. You can apologize for yelling, but if your child broke the rules, you don't need to apologize for being angry. Your child may be sensitive, but this doesn't mean that they are weak. They are strong and resilient and will get over it. You are doing your best. That's all anyone can ask of any parent.

Intimate Relationship with an Empath

Does your partner know that they are an empath or do you think that they might be? If your partner doesn't realize that they are an empath, open up the discussion. Ask them to do the exercise "Am I an Empath?" explained in Chapter 1.

If your intimate partner is an empath, you will receive more love and compassion that you could imagine. But you will also have some lonely nights and a partner who would rather stay at home than attend social events. Empaths need time alone to decompress, and sometimes physical touch or simply proximity is just too much for them to handle. It's up to you if the positives of being with your empathic partner outweigh the negatives.

If you cannot handle being with an empath, leave respectfully and compassionately. Don't be accusatory. If you can't handle the time your partner needs to spend alone, be honest about it. Don't place blame on them for leaving you alone. You simply have different needs that cannot be reconciled.

Be prepared to give up some privacy. Empaths cannot help but to pick up on your emotions and absorb your energy. You should not expect them to keep up their shields at all times, especially when they are at home. This is where they should be able to relax, decompress, and truly be themselves.

Encourage your partner to practice self-care and participate yourself. If they are eating an organic, raw food diet, give it a try, but only after consulting with your doctor. Do yoga or meditate together. Go on long walks in nature. Plant a garden. Get plenty of sleep. When you do these together, don't try to fill every moment with chatter. Embrace silence and doing things mindfully.

Don't bother lying to empaths. They will know. Even if they are not claircognizant or intuitive empaths, they know you well enough to tell what emotions you experience when you lie. Remember, empaths are experts at reading body language, without even doing so consciously. They can't help it, and should not have to.

Love an empath, love their pet. Empaths, especially animal empaths have special bonds with their pet. If your partner is an animal empath, accept that you might never again leave the house without fur on your clothes. Don't ask empaths to choose between you and their pet. It is not a fair request, and you may not like the answer.

Don't expect an empath to change. Empaths are sensitive and prone to hurt feelings—this is not something that they can control. It will be up to you to control your reactions. If you are in an argument, take time to calm down and productively express yourself instead of lashing out.

Argue with compassion. No relationship is perfect. You will argue, you will disagree. Do your best not to yell or lash out with hurtful statements that you will later regret. Approach arguments with the mindset that you want to improve the relationship and move it forward. It doesn't matter who is right and who is wrong.

Support your partner's need to cut some energy vampires out of their life or to create boundaries with others. Boundaries can be difficult for empaths because of their desire to help people and dread of hurting them. If you help your partner to build and maintain these boundaries, they will be healthier, happier, and a better partner. Be understanding when they feel guilty about these boundaries. Remind your partner why boundaries are important. If you have a friend that your partner experiences as an energy vampire, you don't need to cut this person out of your life, but do your best to keep them separated from your partner. Socialize with them outside of your home and don't encourage them to just stop by.

Accept that your partner has boundaries, even with you. No matter how close your bond, empaths will always need some time and space to be alone. You cannot take this personally; it has nothing to do with you. Allowing empaths to spend time alone to relax will allow them to be better partners when they return. If you cohabitate, encourage your partner to make a space in the home that is just theirs. This is where they can retreat when they need to be alone and decompress. Be respectful and stay out of it. Fight the temptation to snoop when they are not home.

It is easy to get complacent with an empath; they will continue to love and support you. But if you want your relationship to thrive, it is important to reciprocate this support, even if they don't ask for it.

Ask your partner questions about their experiences as an empath. Keep an open mind about what they tell you; they will be able to sense if you doubt them! Empaths have often been made to feel weird or ashamed of their abilities. Make sure they know that you don't feel that way. You accept them exactly as they are. They are safe in the relationship to be themselves. Tell them verbally and try to project the emotion to them as well.

Be honest about what you need. You are just as important in the relationship as your empathic partner. Compromise is an integral part of any relationship.

Chapter 9:
Affirmations for Empaths

In this chapter you'll find two guided meditation sessions designed specifically for empaths and highly sensitive people.

In a the next page I have prepared a series of positive affirmations that will help you accept yourself as an empath and strengthen your abilities and qualities.

You can meditate in your head or speak each affirmation aloud. You can even sing them or choose what feels best for you and is appropriate to your situation.

If you feel that negative thoughts are covering your mind while doing your affirmations, just try to relax, focus on your breath, dismiss them, and continue.

To amplify the positive effects of these guided meditations, I recommend to do these exercises daily. However, don't criticize yourself if you don't have time to do your affirmations for a day or even a week.

Let's do some affirmations together!

Guided Meditation 1

I deserve to feel the love I give.

It is OK to have boundaries.

I don't have to fix everyone. I don't have to fix everything.

I release all emotions but my own.

I know what plants need.

My sensitivity makes me stronger.

My abilities are a blessing.

My energetic boundaries are pure and strong.

I willingly free myself from emotions that are not mine to carry.

I am happy being me and appreciate my gift.

It is OK for me to release emotions that are not mine.

I express my needs and desires to supportive people.

I am the one responsible for saving myself, and I know that I can do it.

I choose to release what is not mine to carry.

I really don't need to fix everything for everyone.

I am in control of how I feel in every situation.

I am strong and positive.

It is OK to say no at the right times.

I will use my abilities to improve my own life and the people I meet.

It is OK to listen to my dreams.

I have the ability to clear all the negative energy from my body.

I can control my gift.

I will listen to my intuition.

I can feel the emotions of animals.

I will support, not fix others.

I deserve to be in a loving relationship that makes me feel comfortable.

I will set healthy boundaries.

I treat myself with love and embrace my gift.

I will learn to accept others for who they are.

I don't have to fix everything for everyone.

I can and will set healthy boundaries.

I will protect my energy from draining people.

I love myself as a highly sensitive person and accept my gift.

I can feel the energies of others, but I don't absorb the energies of others.

I am willing to feel only my energy.

I am willing to let go all energy that is not mine.

I can attract gentle relationships into my life.

I feel safe and protected in my life.

I can't save the entire world and everyone in it.

It is safe for me to express my authentic self with the people around me.

It is OK to choose how I want to feel in every situation.

I am willing to feel only my energy.

I am willing to let go all energy that is not mine.

I can attract gentle relationships into my life.

I feel safe and protected in my life.

I can't save the entire world and everyone in it.

It is safe for me to express my authentic self with the people around me.

I give myself permission to release negative emotions which no longer serve me.

I listen to my dreams.

I will support, not fix others.

I deserve to be in a loving relationship that makes me feel comfortable.

I will find balance in my life.

I can say "no" at the right times.

I can ask and receive all the help I need.

I appreciate my abilities everyday.

I fully embrace my wellness, both physical, spiritual and emotional.

I am strong and positive.

It is OK to say no at the right times.

I will use my abilities to improve my own life and the people I meet.

It is OK to listen to my dreams.

I am way stronger than I know.

I will treasure myself.

EMPATH

I will not try to hide my gift.

I choose to release what is not mine to feel.

I respect other people's feelings, but they are not my business.

I know that good things are coming my way,

I am healthy and full of positive energy.

I only welcome uplifting and positive vibrations in my life.

I can feel safe sharing my authentic self with the people around me.

I am the one responsible for saving myself, and I know that I can do it.

I choose to release what is not mine to carry.

I really don't need to fix everything for everyone.

I am in control of how I feel in every situation.

I am strong and positive.

It is OK to say no at the right times.

I will use my abilities to improve my own life and the people I meet.

It is OK to listen to my dreams.

My energetic boundaries are pure and strong.

I willingly free myself from emotions that are not mine to carry.

I am happy being me and appreciate my gift.

It is OK for me to release emotions that are not mine.

I express my needs and desires to supportive people.

I have the ability to clear all the negative energy from my body.

Guided Meditation 2

I am the one responsible for saving myself, and I know that I can do it.

I am way stronger than I know.

I really don't need to fix everything for everyone.

It is safe for me to express my authentic self with the people around me.

I deserve to be in a loving relationship that makes me feel comfortable.

It is OK to listen to my dreams.

I am in control of how I feel in every situation.

It is OK to choose how I want to feel in every situation.

I know that some boundaries are healthy and it is OK to have them.

I am strong and positive.

I will listen to my dreams and follow them.

My abilities are a blessing.

I can ask and receive all the help I need.

I treat myself with love and embrace my gift.

I am willing to feel only my energy.

EMPATH

I can feel the emotions of animals and plants around me.

I am in control of how I feel in every situation.

I set healthy boundaries and this makes me feel better.

I will use my abilities to improve my own life and the people I meet.

I love myself as a highly sensitive person and accept my gift.

I am healthy and full of positive energy.

My sensitivity makes me stronger.

I don't have to fix everything.

I release all the negative emotions which no longer serve me.

I it is completely OK to set healthy boundaries.

I will use my abilities to improve my own life and the people I meet.

I really don't need to fix everything for everyone.

It is OK to say no at the right times.

It is OK to listen to my dreams.

I feel safe, I feel protected and happy.

I can't save the entire world and everyone in it.

I truly deserve to feel the love I give.

I willingly free myself from emotions that are not mine to carry.

I will protect my energy from draining people.

I will find balance in my life.

I respect other people's feelings, but they are not my business.

I don't have to fix everything for everyone.

I will support, not fix others.

I will learn to accept others for who they are.

I only welcome uplifting and positive vibrations in my life.

I can control my gift and channel my energy to spread love and positive feelings.

I choose to release what is not mine to feel.

I will support, not fix others.

I choose to listen to my dreams.

It is OK to say no at the right times.

I know that good things are coming my way,

I am willing to let go all energy that is not mine.

I choose to embrace my wellness, both physical, spiritual and emotional.

I am strong and positive.

I can attract gentle relationships into my life.

It is OK to say no at the right times.

I willingly free myself from emotions that are not mine to carry.

I am happy being me and appreciate my gift.

I will treasure myself.

It is OK for me to release emotions that are not mine.

It is safe for me to express my authentic self with the people around me.

I will use my abilities to improve my own life and the people I meet.

I release all emotions but my own.

I deserve to be in a loving relationship that makes me feel comfortable.

I am happy being me and appreciate my gift.

I appreciate my abilities everyday.

I am strong and positive.

I feel positive and uplifting vibrations in my life.

I express my needs and desires to supportive people.

I am willing to feel only my energy.

I feel safe and protected in my life.

I can't save the entire world and everyone in it.

I am willing to let go all energy that is not mine.

My energetic boundaries are strong and pure.

I express my needs and desires to supportive people.

I have the ability to clear all the negative energy from my body.

I can attract gentle relationships into my life.

It is OK for me to release emotions that are not mine.

I will listen to my intuition.

I can say "no" at the right times.

I can feel safe sharing my authentic self with the people around me.

I can clear all the negative energy from my body.

I will not try to hide my gift.

I can feel the energies of others, but I don't absorb the energies of others.

My energetic boundaries are pure and strong.

I choose to release what is not mine to carry.

Conclusion

Thanks for making it through to the end of *Empath: A Practical Guide for Highly Sensitive People to Control Your Emotions, Overcome Your Fears, Deal with Energy Vampires, and Embrace Your Gift*. Let's hope it was informative and able to provide you with all of the tools you need to achieve your goals whatever they may be.

"The plain truth is that the planet . . . does need desperately more peacemakers, healers, restorers, storytellers, and lovers of every shape and form."

David W. Orr, <u>Ecological Literacy: Educating Our Children for a Sustainable World</u>

The next step is to continue on the adventure that is your life! There is no debating that embracing and developing your empathic abilities can be a difficult path, but it opens up your world beyond what the average person could imagine. Your abilities will allow you to experience and connect with the world on a profound level. You have a unique ability to affect positive change in yourself, the lives of your family and friends, the local community, and even the world.

You embody positive energy. Unfortunately, the world is filled not only with joy but also enormous amounts of suffering. When empaths embrace their abilities and project them into the world, it makes the world a better place. Remember that the next time you're told that you are too sensitive by a Controlling Energy Vampire. You have the strength to make the world a better place.

Take care of yourself. Take care of others. Protect yourself so that you don't make the suffering of others your own. Embrace your talents and strength to help others alleviate their suffering.

Trust yourself. Listen to what your intuition tells you. You will find the answers you actively seek. Use your gifts to focus, listen, and learn. You might not get the answers immediately and they may not be the answers you expect, but they will come.

Finally, if you find this book useful in any way, head over to Amazon and tell me what you think!

Made in the USA
Middletown, DE
25 August 2022